Developments in the European Union

January - June 1995

European Communities Number 12 (1995)

*Presented to Parliament by the Secretary of State
for Foreign and Commonwealth Affairs
by Command of Her Majesty
November 1995*

254939

Cm 3130   LONDON : HMSO   £9.65 net

Contents

Contents

*Note: Sterling/ECU conversions shown in this publication
            are at the 30 June 1995 market rate of £1 = 1.1877
            unless otherwise stated.*

1. Introduction and Summary

1.1 Major developments under the French Presidency included:

- **Enlargement.** Austria, Finland and Sweden joined the European Union on 1 January. The Cannes European Council reaffirmed that accession negotiations for Cyprus and Malta would begin six months after the end of the IGC. Romania and Slovakia submitted formal applications for EU membership (Chapter 8). As part of the pre-accession strategy, the Commission prepared a substantial White Paper on preparation for integration of Associated CEEs into the Internal Market (Chapter 7).

- **Institutional Issues.** The Study Group, which will prepare for the 1996 Inter-Governmental Conference, began working in June and has met regularly since then with a view to producing a final report for the Madrid European Council (Chapter 2).

- **External Affairs.** Activity in this area continued to be dominated by the EU contribution towards a negotiated settlement in the former Yugoslavia (Chapter 3).

- **Justice and Home Affairs.** Agreement on the Europol Convention, the Customs Information System Convention and the Convention on the Protection of the Financial Interests of the Community was reached at the Cannes European Council and all three were subsequently signed on 26 July. A Convention on Simplified Extradition was agreed and signed on 10 March (Chapter 4).

- **Subsidiarity and Deregulation.** The Cannes European Council noted the report from the "Molitor Group" which had been established to examine the impact of Community and National Legislation on Employment and Competitiveness. The Council tasked the Commission to bring forward specific deregulatory measures by the end of the year. A joint Anglo-German report was also submitted to the Commission and other EU Governments contributing to the work in this area. The European Council also noted an interim Commission report on subsidiarity; a full annual report will be presented to the Madrid European Council (Chapter 5).

- **Fight against Fraud.** The Commission published its anti-fraud programme and the sixth annual report on the Fight against Fraud (Chapter 6).

- **Trade and Aid.** The World Trade Organisation entered into force on 1 January. Negotiation of the mid-term review of the fourth Lomé Convention was completed on 30 June, paving the way for signature in November 1995 (Chapter 8).

- **Agriculture, Fisheries and Food.** Agreement was reached on a comprehensive framework of law covering the transport of animals throughout the Community and on the dispute between the Community and Canada which had arisen over the Greenland halibut fishery in the waters of the North-West Atlantic Fisheries Organisation. Ceilings were agreed on fishing effort to apply in Western Waters from 1 January 1996 as part of the arrangements for the integration of Spain and Portugal into the Common Fisheries Policy (Chapter 9).

1.2   Important developments in other areas including, industrial affairs, social affairs, transport and the environment are fully covered in this White Paper.

2. Institutional Issues

Messina Commemoration

2.1   A meeting of Foreign Ministers and representatives of the Commission and European Parliament was held in Messina, Sicily, on 2 June to commemorate the 40th anniversary of the Messina Conference. (The 1955 Messina Conference paved the way for the Treaty of Rome).

1996 IGC Study Group

2.2   The first meeting of the Study Group - established by the Corfu European Council to prepare the 1996 Inter-Governmental Conference (IGC) - was held on 2-3 June in Messina. The Study Group will continue to meet regularly until the Madrid European Council in December 1995. Mr Davis represents the Foreign Secretary in the Study Group. The Cannes European Council confirmed that the mandate of the Study Group is to prepare a series of options for the institutional development of the European Union, and to present these to the Madrid European Council.

2.3   The following subjects were set out for discussion at the IGC by the Maastricht Treaty: the pillared structure; defence; the co-decision procedure; and new Community chapters on energy, civil protection and tourism.

2.4   Since then other areas for discussion have been added to this list: the budgetary provisions for the Treaty; the College of Commissioners; Qualified Majority Voting procedures; and the implications of enlargement to the East and South.

2.5   Any member state is free to add further issues to the agenda.

3. Common Foreign and Security Policy (CFSP)

Bosnia

3.1 The war in Bosnia remained the major focus of CFSP activity. The European Union continued its contribution to efforts to find a peaceful and negotiated settlement, and to ensure the implementation of sanctions as a means of increasing pressure on the Serbs to end the war. The European Union also maintained its humanitarian relief programmes in the Former Yugoslavia, including the administration of Mostar at the request of the Bosnian Federation.

Other International Issues

3.2 Within the framework of CFSP the Foreign Affairs Council and the Political Committee regularly discussed and coordinated approaches to a number of important international issues including Chechnya, Croatia, Rwanda, Burundi and the Middle East Peace Process.

Joint Actions/Common Positions

3.3 The European Union continued to adopt and implement *Joint Actions* and *Common Positions* covering a wide range of international issues. The CFSP instruments adopted under Articles J2 and J3 during the period are;

- a joint action on anti-personnel mines - providing for a moratorium on anti-personnel mine exports; a contribution of c£2.5 million by the EU to the UN Voluntary Trust Fund for mine clearance; and coordinated preparation for the 1980 Convention Review Conference on strengthening restrictions on anti-personnel mines.

- a common position on Burundi - aiming to restore confidence in Burundi by promoting dialogue between the Government and the people, and providing humanitarian aid.

Ongoing Joint actions and Common Positions include:

- humanitarian aid to Bosnia - £85 million has been committed by the EU since January 1995;

- the EU Administration of Mostar - EU budget for this year is £68 million;

- promotion of the Stability Pact - finally adopted in March 1995;

- action in support of the Middle East Peace Process: including the Council decision to set in motion and organise the election monitoring exercise; and

- lobbying for an extension of the Non-Proliferation Treaty.

The EU also produced 64 statements/declarations relating to 37 countries under the framework of CFSP. These included statements setting out the stance of member states towards the conflicts in ex-Yugoslavia and Chechnya, human rights in Nigeria and the fatwa on Salman Rushdie.

3.4   A further focus was the development of relations, under the Anglo-Italian initiative, with the nine Central European countries which have Europe Agreements. See Chapter 8 also.

4. Justice and Home Affairs

Europol

4.1   The Cannes European Council on 26-27 June reached agreement on the text of the Convention to create the European Police Office, Europol. The Convention was signed by member states' representatives in Brussels on 26 July.

4.2   The Council agreed to settle within twelve months the question of a possible jurisdiction for the European Court of Justice in the settlement of disputes. Work will now be taken forward on the drafting of supplementary regulations and rules of procedure which need to be in place before Europol begins its work.

Customs Co-operation

4.3   The Cannes European Council finalised the text of the Customs Information System (CIS) Convention, which is aimed at assisting - through the rapid dissemination between member states of information and intelligence - the prevention, investigation and prosecution of serious breaches of national laws concerning, in particular illicit drug trafficking and the prohibition and restriction of imports, exports and goods in transit.

4.4   The CIS Convention was signed in Brussels on 26 July.

Immigration and Asylum

4.5   The Justice and Home Affairs Council on 9-10 March agreed the texts of a Regulation on a uniform format for visas and a Resolution on minimum guarantees for asylum seekers.

4.6   At its meeting on 20-21 June the Council adopted a Recommendation on harmonising means of combatting illegal immigration and illegal employment, and concluded negotiations on a Resolution on burden sharing of temporarily displaced persons.

Extradition

4.7   The Convention on Simplified Extradition Procedures, which will accelerate the surrender process for a person who consents to be extradited, was signed at the Justice and Home Affairs Council on 9-10 March. Work continues on the development of a convention to simplify extradition conditions in non-consent cases.

Fraud against the Community budget

4.8   The European Council on 26-27 June concluded the first-stage Convention on the Protection of the Financial Interests of the Community, which sets out minimum standards to be met by all member states for the protection of Community funds under national criminal law. The Convention was signed on 26 July.

4.9   The parallel First Pillar Regulation on administrative penalties was agreed at ECOFIN on 17 June.

Drugs

4.10   The Cannes European Council approved work on the draft EU Action Plan to Combat Drugs and the guidelines adopted for the Community programme on the prevention of drug dependence. It urged member states to ensure practical implementation of the strategy, including reducing supply, combatting trafficking and international co-operation and instructed that a group of experts submit proposals for dealing with these issues to the Madrid European Council in December.

Racism and Xenophobia

4.11   The final report of the Consultative Commission was considered by the European Council in Cannes. The report included a large number of recommendations covering a wide range of policy areas, most of which will receive further consideration in the relevant Council committees and working groups. The Council concluded that the Consultative Commission should reconvene to study the feasibility of a European Monitoring Centre on Racism and Xenophobia.

Title VI Financing

4.12   The Justice and Home Affairs Council on 20-21 June agreed a mechanism for funding operational activity in the Third Pillar (such as training, seminars and research), drawing on the provision allocated to justice and home affairs co-operation in the 1995 Community budget. Member states are required to submit proposals for projects to the Commission, which will then prepare bids for consideration and selection by a working party of member states' representatives.

5. Subsidiarity and Deregulation

Subsidiarity

5.1   The European Council in December 1994 remitted the Commission to submit proposals for completion of its review of existing legislation. The Commission presented a short report to the Cannes European Council on 26-27 June. It will present a full, annual report to the Madrid European Council in December 1995. The June report recognised the continuing importance of the principle of subsidiarity and committed the Commission to ensuring that it is fully respected in the Community's legislative process. The report describes new Commission internal procedures for ensuring that subsidiarity is taken properly into account in the preparation of legislative proposals.

5.2   As evidence of progress, the report draws attention to:

- a continuing reduction in the number of major legislative proposals;

- implementation of a programme agreed at the European Council in December 1992, to withdraw or revise a large number of legislative proposals;

- implementation of the review of existing legislation, which the Commission began in 1993. The report mentions Commission proposals for the adaptation or simplification of legislation in a number of areas, including 37 directives in the transport and veterinary fields.

5.3   In discussions with the Commission and other member states, the UK Government continued to emphasise the importance it attaches to ensuring that subsidiarity is firmly embedded in the Community legislative process. The UK welcomed the progress made by the Commission. But it expressed concern that the Commission continued to make a number of proposals which, in whole or in part, were inconsistent with subsidiarity.

5.4   The Study Group set up to prepare for the 1996 Inter-Governmental Conference held a number of discussions on subsidiarity. All member states agreed on the importance of the principle. The group will discuss ways of developing the operation of subsidiarity to make it more effective in practice.

5.5   The Cannes European Council considered the Commission's report and progress more generally. The Council conclusions reiterated the importance the Council attaches to rigorous implementation of subsidiarity and called on the Commission to complete implementation of the 1993 review of existing legislation as soon as possible and to report back to the European Council in December 1995.

5.6   The UK, working with the Commission and other member states, will continue to press for progress in implementing subsidiarity. The UK attaches particular importance to satisfactory follow-up to the remits agreed by the European Council.

Deregulation

5.7   There is growing evidence that both Governments and businesses throughout Europe now recognise the importance of deregulation to the long-term prosperity of its citizens. The Cannes European Council noted the need to combat excessive regulation in order to stimulate employment, competitiveness and innovation. The European Council also mandated the Commission to propose specific measures to take deregulation forward by the end of the year. Commission President Jacques Santer has declared his wish to see the Commission taking "less action, but better action". The Commission have made a commitment to prepare a report for the Madrid European Council in December.

5.8   European policy in this area is underpinned by a number of recent studies which have strengthened the link between deregulation and improving the competitiveness of industry throughout the Community.

5.9   The Molitor Group of independent experts, established by the Commission following the Corfu Council, has examined the impact of existing Community legislation on competitiveness and employment, and submitted a report to the Cannes Council. The report makes many detailed and sensible proposals for deregulation in the areas of environment, health and safety, food hygiene, machine standards and small and medium sized enterprises. Disappointingly, the report also makes proposals on employment law that are regulatory rather than deregulatory. These proposals would destroy jobs and have been opposed both by key business members of the Molitor Group and by the Government, the Confederation of British Industry and by the Union of Industrial and Employers Confederation of Europe (UNICE).

5.10   The Anglo-German Group of senior UK/German businessmen established following last year's Summit between the Prime Minister and Chancellor Kohl, published its 'Deregulation Now' report in March. The report contains a series of recommendations covering chemical, food production/distribution, transport and cross sectoral issues. The report also makes some specific recommendations on improving EC regulatory systems, including a deregulation checklist.

5.11   Following the Anglo-German Summit on 26 May 1995 a joint letter covering the Anglo-German Deregulation Group report was sent by the Prime Minister and Chancellor Kohl to Commission President Santer and EU heads of Government urging them to give the report's proposals serious consideration.

5.12   Both the Molitor Report and the Anglo-German Report advance the case for more general reforms aimed at both reducing, and checking the flow of, unnecessary regulation. Specific recommendations include:

- clear leadership on deregulation within the Commission;

- greater business consultation;

- regulatory checklists to improve the quality of EC legislation and strengthened systems to assess the impact of new proposals on employment, competitiveness and innovation;

- a coherent programme of action on deregulation.

The Government will make its views known on both reports to the Commission in advance of the Madrid European Council.

5.13   The UNICE report on the regulatory burdens faced by European business, commissioned by DGIII, was published on 12 October, following an earlier interim report in June. The study's conclusions, based on pan-European research covering 2,500 companies (80 per cent of which were SMEs) are that companies view the current level of regulation in Europe as an impediment to competitiveness which imposes substantial hidden costs on business. The UNICE report provides valuable additional evidence in support of our deregulatory objectives.

5.14   DGXXIII's Administrative Simplification Committee held its first forum on improving the regulatory environment for business in June. Around 250 people attended the forum, which focused on the identification of regulatory best practice for start-ups and businesses in their early years. The forum made a valuable and positive contribution to the debate on legislative and administrative simplification in Europe, and demonstrated the extent to which this is a common concern shared by administrations and business alike across the Community. Subsequent fora will focus on best practice for the growth and transfer stages of the business life-cycle.

6. Economic, Budgetary and Monetary Matters

Supplementary Budget No 1 for 1995

*Converted at the rate of £1 = 1.2705 ecu, which is the rate set for UK VAT and Fourth Resource Contributions to the 1995 Community Budget.

6.1   On 14 February, the Commission proposed a preliminary draft supplementary and amending budget (PDSAB). The proposal allocated to individual budget headings the funds for enlargement included in the 1995 budget. It also reduced agricultural requirements by 1,028.5 million ecu (£809.5 million) based on the latest forecasts. On the revenue side, the PDSAB budgetised the balance of unused payment appropriations from the 1994 budget resulting in a net reduction of 5,500 million ecu (£4,329 million*) in the call-up of own resources from member states. It also updated the 1991 and 1994 figures for the United Kingdom abatement, reducing it in the 1995 budget by 340 million ecu (£268 million*) to 1,533 million ecu (£1,207 million*). Following consideration by the Council, the PDSAB No 1 for 1995 was formally adopted by the European Parliament on 26 April.

1996 Budget

6.2   On 15 June, the Commission published its Preliminary Draft Budget (PDB) for 1996. The Commission's proposals respect the commitment ceiling for each category of expenditure agreed by the Edinburgh European Council in December 1992. The PDB is within the existing own resources ceiling of 1.20 per cent of Community Gross National Product. Commitment appropriations in the PDB total 86,280 million ecu (£72,645 million), 8.06 per cent above the 1995 budget, as amended by the supplementary budget No.1). The total for payment appropriations is 81,928 million ecu (£68,980 million), an increase of 8.60 per cent over 1995. The total for payment appropriations represents 1.197 per cent of Community GNP, including "other revenue". The budget for 1996 will be considered by the budgetary authority (Council and European Parliament) and is due to be adopted in December.

Revision to the Financial Perspective

6.3   On 10 March, the Commission presented two proposals for technical adjustments to the Financial Perspective as permitted by the Inter-Institutional Agreement (IIA) of 29 October 1993. The Commission sought a technical adjustment to reflect movements in Community GNP and prices. This adjustment will be taken into account by the Council in adopting a Draft Budget for 1996. The

Commission also sought an adjustment to take account of the underutilisation of commitment appropriations in the structural funds in 1994 by transferring commitments and payments into 1996 and 1997 and increasing payments in 1996 to ensure an orderly progression of payments in relation to commitments. This proposal was considered at a meeting of the Trialogue (Council, European Parliament, and Commission) on 4 April where a more even split for commitments in 1996 and 1997 and a reduced increase in payments in 1996 were agreed.

Commission Financial Management

6.4   At ECOFIN on 20 March, Commissioner Liikanen gave an outline of a Commission internal work programme to strenghen the management of the Union's financial resources. He explained that the programme, which is underway, would have three stages:

- **consolidation:** which identifies measures which can be taken within the framework of existing regulations;

- **reform:** including a review of the regulatory framework and proposals for amendment to ensure rigorous and transparent financial management; and

- **reinforced partnership with the member states:** in recognition that, without denying the overall responsibility of the Commission, 80 per cent of Community funds are spent by the member states.

Fraud against the Community Budget

On 20 February, the Commission presented its new anti-fraud work programme for 1995 to ECOFIN. The anti-fraud work programme arises from the Commission's anti-fraud strategy, published on 24 March 1994. On 29 March, the Commission published its sixth annual report on the Fight Against Fraud which reviews the progress made in 1994. On 19 June, ECOFIN underlined the importance of waging war on fraud and the need for close co-operation between the Commission and member states. It also stressed the importance of clear, simple and enforceable legislation.

In line with the conclusions of the Essen European Council in December 1994, ECOFIN considered on 19 June the issue of member states' reports on national measures to combat fraud, waste and mismanagement of Community funds. It agreed to further examination of member states' reports in advance of their submission to the December European Council.

Following further detailed discussion during the first half of 1995, the Council reached a common position on 29 June on the draft Council Regulation on the protection of the Community's financial interests. The Council will consult the European Parliament before reaching its decision.

Court of Auditors' Reports on the 1992 and 1993 Budgets

6.5   The Court of Auditors' report, which was published on 24 November 1994, was considered by ECOFIN on 20 March. ECOFIN adopted a recommendation which was transmitted to the European Parliament. The recommendation included a request for the Commission to report back by November 1995 on the steps taken to overcome the deficiencies identified by the Court and by the Council in its recommendation. On 5 April, the European Parliament granted a discharge to the Commission in respect of its implementation of the 1993 budget. It also granted discharge on the 1992 budget, following receipt of additional information from the Commission.

European Monetary System (EMS) and Exchange Rate Mechanism (ERM)

6.6   Austria, Finland and Sweden joined the EMS on 1 January. Austria joined the ERM on 9 January.

6.7   On 6 March, the bilateral central rates of the Spanish peseta against other ERM currencies were reduced by 7 per cent, and those of the Portuguese escudo by 3.5 per cent.

European Monetary Union (EMU)

6.8   On 31 May, the Commission published a Green Paper on the practical arrangements for the introduction of the single currency.

6.9   EMU was discussed by ECOFIN on 19 June and the European Council at Cannes on 26-27 June. At Cannes, Heads of Government effectively ruled out a move to Stage 3 of EMU in 1997. In the Council Conclusions, Heads of Government commissioned ECOFIN to do further work on defining a reference scenario for EMU, with a view to reporting back to the Madrid European Council in December. The Council also requested that ECOFIN examine the future relationship between participant countries in EMU and other member states.

Broad Economic Guidelines

6.10   In accordance with Article 103(2) of the Treaty, the Cannes European Council approved a draft Recommendation for the Broad Guidelines of the economic policies of the member states and of the Community, as submitted by ECOFIN on 19 June. (The final non-binding recommendation setting out the broad guidelines were adopted by ECOFIN on 10 July). The Council's recommendation sets out the main economic objectives of sustainable non-inflationary and employment-creating growth. It covers policies directed at price stability, sound public finances and structural reform. The guidelines will inform the monitoring of economic developments and policies in member states in the context of the multilateral surveillance exercises required under Article 103(3) of the Treaty.

Excessive deficits

6.11   ECOFIN on 19 June agreed that the three new member states had excessive deficits. (The United Kingdom's excessive deficits decision - agreed by ECOFIN on 19 September 1994, under Article 104c.6 of the Treaty - stands until abrogated). As a result the UK and eleven other member states all (except Ireland, Luxembourg and Germany, whose excessive deficit was abrogated at the June ECOFIN) have an excessive deficit. Having established the existence of an excessive deficit, Article 104c.7 of the Treaty provides that the Council shall make recommendations to the member state concerned " ... with a view to bringing that situation (ie the excessive deficit) to an end within a given period". (These recommendations are updated each year and were discussed at later Council meetings in July).

United Kingdom Convergence Programme - March Update

6.12   On 9 March, the UK submitted a further update of its May 1993 convergence programme to the Commission. The projections in the update were consistent with the Financial Statement and Budget Report and took account of the measures announced in the November 1994 Budget. It also took account of the additional package of measures announced on 8 December, following the decision to leave the rate of VAT on domestic fuel and power unchanged at 8 per cent. The update informs the multilateral surveillance discussions that take place during the year.

Loans to Central and Eastern Europe

6.13   On 20 March, ECOFIN agreed criteria and geographical priorities for EU macro-financial assistance to third countries. In future, such external loans will be made primarily to countries with which the EU maintains close political and economic links. The May ECOFIN Council approved the disbursement of the 85 million ecu (£72 million) macro-financial assistance loan to Ukraine agreed in December 1994,and agreed in principle on a further loan to Ukraine of up to 200 million ecu (£168 million). The Ukraine loan is conditional on continued progress with the Standby Arrangement with the IMF, adequate burdensharing with other donors of this, and progress on nuclear safety. At the April ECOFIN Council, macro-financial assistance to Belarus of up to 75 million ecu (£63million) was egreed. The disbursement of this loan is conditional on a Standby Arrangement which has not yet been agreed with the IMF.

Investor Compensation Directive

6.14 ECOFIN reached political agreement for a common position on this directive which will require up to at least 20,000 ecu (£16,839) of an investor's assets to be protected if an investment firm or credit institution fails. The directive, which is now closely modelled on the Deposit Guarantee Directive, assigns primary responsibility for compensation to a firm's home state scheme, so aligning it with responsibility for authorisation. The directive is to enter into force 18 months after final adoption. The UK Investor Compensation Scheme already exceeds the requirements of the directive in many respects.

UCITS Amending Directive

6.15 ECOFIN has suspended work on this directive which aims to extend and refine the 1985 Directive on Undertakings for Collective Investment in Transferable Securities. (This currently covers roughly half of the UK unit trusts and the forthcoming open ended investment companies). The extensions included feeder funds, cash funds, and funds of UCITS. The Council has invited the Commission to consider revising its proposal because it has been found to contain technical flaws and because it does not seem possible to reach a qualified majority for a common position on it.

Carbon/Energy Tax

6.16 The Commission presented to ECOFIN in May a revision to their 1992 proposal for a carbon/energy tax. This was remitted to an ad hoc group for detailed consideration. The Government recognises that those member states who wish to introduce national taxes on carbon/energy should be free to do so. The Government is therefore prepared to consider a framework which ensures that such taxes are consistent with the single market. The Commission's proposals go beyond this.

Statistics relating to Trading of Goods

6.17 Council Regulation (EC) No 1172/95 of 22 May 1995 governs the collection and compilation of trade statistics relating to trading of goods between member states of the Community and third countries. It supersedes Council Regulation (EEC) No 1736/75 of 14 July 1975 and its amendments. Regulation 1172/95 revises the provisions of the former Regulation, 1736/75, apart from intra Community aspects, which are covered by Council Regulation 3330/91 and its implementing regulations, governing Intrastat. As Council Regulation 1172/95 revises existing legislation, no national legislation is required to implement Community procedures. In response to representation from the UK and other member states, the Commission agreed that the new regulation would not impose any new obligations on business and the main source of statistical information would be provided by customs documentation. The new regulation allows for the collection of statistics to be extended to transit, customs warehouses, free zones and free warehouses: following strong representation from the UK and other member states the regulation made such provision optional enabling member states wishing to collect such information to do so; the UK has not taken up the option. Although Council Regulation 1172/95 has entered into force, its actual application is dependent on the supporting implementating Commission Regulation, which is expected to enter into force in 1995.

7. Making the Single Market Work

7.1   The Presidency held an informal meeting of Internal Market ministers on 10 March, and an Internal Market Council on 6 June. The main issues of this period were: extension of the internal market to the Central and East Europeans and maximising the benefits of the Single Market.

Preparation for Integration of Associated CEEs into the Internal Market.

7.2   A substantial White Paper on this subject, prepared by the Commission, received a positive welcome from the Council. This was followed by a meeting of the Ministers of the associated countries with their EU counterparts, where the challenge of adapting legislation and administrative structures was greeted with enthusiasm, as it is seen as an essential part of the accession process. The major practical follow-up for the Commission will be the establishment of a Technical Assistance and Information Exchange Office, which will serve as a central coordination point for advising the CEEs over the next few years.

Making the Single Market Work

7.3   As well as discussion of the state of transposition of legislation, and the Commission's publication of its latest Annual Report, the Council dealt with two key items:

- **Effective uniform application of Community law** was the subject of a Commission Communication, then a Council Resolution adopted in June. The focus is on penalties for breaches of internal market rules; the Council agreed that the absence of "effective, proportionate and dissuasive" national penalty provisions could endanger the even application, and therefore the smooth operation, of the Single Market across the Union. A system of transparency will help the Commission to verify that national provisions are equally effective. Where they are not, the Commission may, if necessary, take action to resolve the situation. Any such action must show "due regard to the respective jurisdictions of the Community and the member states and for the principles of national laws, in the light of the subsidiarity and proportionality principles".

- The Council held negotiations on the **exchange of information on national measures derogating from the principle of free movement of goods.** A common position was reached on the draft decision. The Decision will bolster full implementation of Article 100B of the Treaty, by obliging member states to notify the Commission of any refusal to apply the mutual recognition principle to products legally manufactured elsewhere in the EU.

7.4   Two significant pieces of legislation were adopted. The lifts directive which aims to remove technical barriers to trade in lifts and lift safety components by harmonising health and safety requirements across the European Community. The Council also reached a common position on the draft data protection directive which seeks to establish a common set of data protection rules throughout the Community in order to ensure the free flow of personal data within the Single Market. On 15 June, the European Parliament proposed seven amendments to the common position.

8. External Relations including Trade and Aid

Enlargement

8.1   Austria, Finland and Sweden became members of the European Union on 1 January.

8.2   At the Foreign Affairs Council on 12-13 June, Europe (Association) Agreements were signed with Estonia, Latvia and Lithuania.

8.3   Two Central European associated states submitted formal applications for EU membership: Romania on 22 June, and Slovakia on 27 June.

8.4   Association Councils were held for the first time with Bulgaria, the Czech Republic, Romania and Slovakia. Second Councils were held with Hungary and Poland. In accordance with the pre-accession strategy agreed at the Essen European Council (December 1994), EU Ministers also met their Central European counterparts to discuss issues across the three pillars. The Cannes European Council agreed to grant aid over the next five years under the Phare programme for the countries of Central and Eastern Europe totalling 6.69 billion ecu (£5.62 billion).

8.5   Also as part of the pre-accession strategy, the Commission prepared a substantial White Paper on preparation for integration of Associated CEEs into the Internal Market. See Chapter 7.

8.6   The Cannes European Council on 26-27 June reaffirmed that accession negotiations for Cyprus and Malta would start six months after the end of the Inter-Governmental Conference, taking into account its conclusions. Separate EU/Malta and EU/Cyprus Association Councils on 12 June agreed pre-accession strategies for both countries, and signed the Fourth Financial Protocol.

Former Soviet Union

8.7   The European Union continued to provide the countries of the former Soviet Union with technical assistance under the TACIS scheme to assist the process of reform.

8.8   Partnership and Co-operation Agreements were signed with Kazakhstan, Kyrgyzstan and Belarus on 23 January, 9 February and 6 March respectively.

8.9   The European Union signed an Interim Agreement on trade with Ukraine on 1 June. The Agreement gives immediate effect to the trade provisions of the Partnership and Co-operation Agreement which was signed on 14 June 1994, pending its ratification.

Transatlantic Relations

8.10   On 14 June, an EU/US Summit meeting in Washington considered ways of enhancing the EU/US relationship and charged a group of senior representatives to report on this issue to the next EU/US Summit at the end of 1995.

8.11   An EU/Canada Summit took place in Halifax on 17 June, at which an EU/Canada Science and Technology Agreement was signed.

8.12   On 29 June, the Council agreed to prolong, until the end of 1995, interim arrangements with the United States to compensate for tariff increases in Austria, Finland and Sweden as a result of their accession to the European Union. The Council also agreed to reduce duties on imports of newsprint as interim compensation to Canada for these tariff increases.

Asia

8.13   An agreement with China on trade in textiles and clothing not covered by the Multi-Fibre Arrangement was concluded at the 23-24 January Foreign Affairs Council. On 6-7 March, the Foreign Affairs Council agreed to increase Community quotas on imports of certain non-textile products from China, inter alia to take account of European Union enlargement.

8.14   On 29-30 May, the Foreign Affairs Council agreed a strategy for developing relations with Japan. An EU/Japan Summit was held in Paris on 19 June.

8.15   A Co-operation Agreement with Vietnam was initialled on 30 May.

8.16   The twelfth session of the Joint Commission with Sri Lanka took place in Brussels on 27-28 June. This was the first session since the EC/Sri Lanka Co-operation Agreement on Partnership and Development came into force in April.

Mediterranean

8.17   At the Foreign Affairs Council on 10-11 April, the Commission presented its proposals for implementing the Euro-Mediterranean partnership. The Cannes European Council endorsed a Presidency report on the Euro-Mediterranean partnership, in preparation for a conference which will take place in Barcelona from 27-28 November.

8.18   At the Foreign Affairs Council on 6-7 March, the Council agreed the terms for Customs Union with Turkey. The proposal was subsequently remitted to the European Parliament for approval.

8.19   Negotiations continued for the conclusion of new Agreements with Morocco, Tunisia, Egypt and Israel. A negotiating mandate for a new agreement with Jordan, similar to those for Morocco, Tunisia and Egypt, was agreed at the Foreign Affairs Council on 12-13 June.

Latin America

8.20   The EU/Central America Ministerial meeting (San Jose XI) was held in Panama City on 23 February. The Fifth Institutionalised Ministerial Meeting between the European Union and the Rio Group was held in Paris on 17 March.

8.21   The European Union and Mexico signed a Joint Solemn Declaration on 2 May in Paris. The EU/Paraguay and EU/Uruguay Joint Commissions were held in Brussels on 22 and 23 June respectively.

8.22   On 12-13 June, the Foreign Affairs Council approved the negotiating mandate for an inter-regional co-operation agreement between the European Union and MERCOSUR (Argentina, Brazil, Paraguay and Uruguay). The negotiating mandate was presented to MERCOSUR on 30 June.

Relations with Developing Countries

8.23   The 1 June Development Council made further progress on the programme established by the Horizon 2000 Declaration on enhancing co-ordination between EC and member states' overseas development policies, and a major joint evaluation of EC programmes was launched. Resolutions were adopted on structural adjustment and regional integration, providing a framework for EC interventions in those sectors. The Council also agreed a political and technical dialogue with Rwanda to enable temporarily-suspended EC aid to be resumed.

8.24   Around 230 million ecu (£193.66 million) of humanitarian aid was approved, primarily for former Yugoslavia (43 per cent) and the countries of the former Soviet Union (29 per cent), as was 940,000 tonnes of food aid for developing countries. The Cannes European

Council agreed to grant aid over the next five years for the non-member countries of the Mediterranean totalling 4.69 billion ecu (£3.94 billion).

The Fourth EC-ACP Convention (Lomé IV)

The Fourth Lomé Convention, signed in 1989, is an aid and trade agreement between the European Community and its 15 member states, and 70 countries in Africa, the Caribbean and the Pacific (ACP). Lomé IV lasts for ten years, with provision for a mid-term review after five years. The negotiation of this mid-term review was completed on 30 June (signature is due in November 1995). The main elements of the review were:

- agreement on the financing package for assistance to the ACP during the second half of Lomé IV (known as the eighth European Development Fund -EDF VIII);

- improved trading arrangements for the ACP (greater access to EC markets for agricultural products and more generous rules of origin and cumulation);

- measures to improve aid effectiveness including the introduction of a human rights suspension clause and tranching of country programme funds.

EU member states pledged 13.307 billion ecu (£11.2 billion) for EDF VIII, representing maintenance in real terms of EDF VII. The mid-term review will provide a strong framework for EU/ACP relations until the end of Lomé IV in the year 2000.

South Africa

8.25   A negotiating mandate for a long-term agreement with South Africa was agreed at the Foreign Affairs Council on 12-13 June. The mandate consists of two elements: an offer to negotiate a Special Protocol to the Lomé Convention giving South Africa a form of qualified membership, and a separate bilateral agreement on trade and co-operation. The mandate also offers 500 million ecu (£420 million) to South Africa over four years for its programme of Reconstruction and Development, and an agreement on Science and Technology to be negotiated separately.

Trade and Investment

8.26   The World Trade Organisation (WTO) entered into

force on 1 January. On 24 March the WTO General Council confirmed the appointment of former Italian Trade Minister Renato Ruggiero, the candidate supported by the European Union, as WTO Director-General. Mr Ruggiero took up his appointment on 1 May.

8.27   On 10-11 April, the Foreign Affairs Council endorsed the launching of negotiations in the Organisation for Economic Co-operation and Development (OECD) on a Multilateral Agreement on Investment. Negotiations were formally launched at the 22-23 May OECD Ministerial meeting.

8.28   WTO negotiations on trade in financial services and the movement of persons were due to be concluded by 30 June. The Cannes European Council stressed the need to conclude these negotiations with a substantive and balanced result. However, there was no agreement by the deadline, and the Foreign Affairs Council, meeting in Geneva on 30 June, endorsed a Commission proposal to prolong the negotiations until 28 July. The WTO Council agreed to the extension, enabling the negotiations to be concluded successfully by the revised deadline.

9. Agriculture, Fisheries and Food

European Agricultural Guidance and Guarantee Fund (EAGGF)

9.1   United Kingdom receipts during the period from the Guarantee section of the (EAGGF) (which funds the Common Agricultural Policy) were £1,653 million. Because of the operation of the system of delayed advances, these receipts relate to expenditure incurred during the period 16 October 1994 to 30 April 1995. Receipts were largely for arable area payments, including set-aside, and ewe and beef premia.

EC Structural Funds

9.2   For the period January - June 1995, United Kingdom receipts from the Guidance section of the EAGGF and from the Financial Instrument for Fisheries Guidance (FIFG) budget amounted to £29.6 million and £0.3 million respectively.

Financial Management of the Common Agricultural Policy (CAP)

9.3   On 22 May, the Council adopted Regulation 1287/95/EC which amended Regulation 729/70 on the financing of the CAP. The regulation which came into force on 16 October (the effective start of the 1996 budget year) amends procedures for clearance of the annual accounts which member states are required to submit to the Commission regarding all transactions funded from the EAGGF Guarantee section. Its aim is to improve the financial management of the CAP by introducing basic standards of control for each paying agency and requiring annual accounts to be certified by independent auditors. This will allow Commission auditors to devote more time to checking member states' controls, with the aim of agreeing rapid improvements where appropriate. Procedures will be speeded up and be more transparent and all information will be held centrally. A major aim is to improve the dialogue between the Commission and the member states. Previously, member states have been protective of their positions in the face of Commission criticism of controls on historic expenditure. There will now be greater focus on agreeing improvements to current practice and the Commission will be spending a greater proportion of its time on compliance audits rather than accounting audits. Current arrangements for CAP administration in the UK can be adapted with little difficulty.

Operation of the Agrimonetary System

9.4   On 1 February, new rules came into force on the operation of the agrimonetary system. The rules for automatically adjusting green rates to keep them in line with market rates of exchange were maintained. However, in order to strengthen the protection for strong currency member states against green rate revaluations (which cut support prices), a delay was introduced before these are implemented. In addition, compensation is available for revaluations which more than offset any previous price rise due to a green rate devaluation.

9.5   Under these rules, revaluations should have taken place from mid-April for certain strong currency member states.   However, due to pressure from these countries and concern over the budget cost of compensating for the revaluations, these were postponed pending a Commission proposal to derogate from the existing rules.

9.6   Agreement on the revised arrangements was reached at the Agriculture Council on 22 June. In the case of green rate revaluations for the strong currencies implemented between 23 June 1995 and 1 January 1996, the green rate applied to all Common Agricultural Policy direct payments (arable area and livestock headage payments, and amounts of a structural or environmental nature) will be frozen at its 23 June level until 1 January 1999. Compensation for income losses due to support price cuts was agreed, to be paid over three years on a degressive basis. This will be part-financed from the Community budget. The UK voted against these arrangements because, although they significantly reduced the cost of potential compensation, they also give rise to differences in the rates of CAP direct payments between member states.

9.7   The agreement cleared the way for revaluations to take place for the strong currency member states. The rules for triggering green rate changes, therefore, reverted to their normal operation on 24 June.

The Welfare of Animals during Transport

In June, after protracted negotiations, the Agriculture Council agreed measures to complete Directive 91/628 on the protection of animals in transit. This was a significant step forward in that, for the first time, Community rules were set on the maximum journey times for which farm livestock may be transported, underpinned by a requirement that, after a journey, farm livestock will have to be allowed at least 24 hours to recover.

The general maximum journey limit for farm livestock - cattle, sheep, goats, pigs and horses - is of eight hours. Livestock may only be transported for longer periods in vehicles which provide specified equipment such as movable pens and adjustable ventilation. Under these conditions, maximum transport times (extendable by up to 2 hours in order to reach the destination) are differentiated according to species, reflecting scientific work:

- adult cattle and sheep: for up to 14 hours before a rest/water/food stop of at least 1 hour. Then for up to a further 14 hours;

- young livestock: for up to 9 hours before a rest/water/ food stop of at least 1 hour. Then for up to a further 9 hours;

- pigs: for up to 24 hours, provided that they have continuous access to water;

- horses: for up to 24 hours, provided that they are given water and, if necessary, food every 8 hours.

The rules include space allowances for different species of livestock in the different types of transport. They also include Community-wide powers to enforce the rules, including a licensing system for transport operators, with member states empowered to prohibit from transporting animals those who commit serious or repeated offences, whether based in the UK or elsewhere in the Community. There are tighter rules on the planning of journeys for intra-Community trade, with examination by officials of plans both before and after a journey. There is also a Commission commitment to increase its supervision of enforcement and an obligation on member states to report annually. Member states have to implement the main provisions of the directive by 31 December 1996, and the limits applying to vehicles not meeting the higher standards by 31 December 1997.

Review of the Directive on the Rearing of Calves

9.8   The Government recognises the concern of the British public that, once exported from the UK, many calves are reared in a close confinement system - the veal crate - and on a diet lacking in fibre, both of which we have prohibited in the UK since 1990. The Community rules on the rearing of calves, which currently permit member states to retain the use of veal crates, were due to be reviewed in 1997. However, the Government successfully pressed for this review to be brought forward to 1995, and the European Commission has asked its scientific experts to prepare a report on the latest scientific advice so that it may be in a position to make proposals for the welfare standards to be applied in future to calves.

Bananas

9.9   Following a petition in September 1994 by the US multinational, Chiquita, the United States Trade Representative (USTR) began a Section 301 investigation into the effects of the Community banana regime on US trade. On 9 January, the USTR made a preliminary determination that the regime adversely affects US commercial interests and has since demanded substantial changes to it. Discussions between the Community and the US took place earlier this year but there were no formal negotiations. The US, supported by Guatemala, Honduras and Mexico, has now formally requested consultations with the Community under the dispute settlement procedures of the World Trade Organisation. The UK has argued that the kind of changes sought by the US would be very damaging to Caribbean producers and is encouraging the Commission to mount a strong defence of the regime in Geneva.

Implementation of the Community's Uruguay Round Agriculture Commitments

9.10   Following changes, agreed in December 1994, to the basic CAP commodity regulations to provide for implementation of the Community's new commitments, responsibility for most aspects of implementation was assigned to the Commission working through Management Committees and the Trade Mechanisms Committee. For most sectors, the new World Trade Organisation obligations on increased access, and cuts in subsidised exports take effect from 1 July 1995, the start of the majority of marketing years. Detailed arrangements, tailored to the circumstances of each commodity, are now in place.

Arable Area Aid: Link Between Market and Structural Set-Aside

9.11   Following sustained pressure from the UK, the June Agriculture Council agreed that eligible arable land taken out of production under the Community agri-environmental and forestry schemes should be allowed to count against a producer's set-aside obligations under the Arable Area Payments Scheme. Council Regulation 1460/95/EC implementing this decision came into force on 1 July. However, the link with set-aside is not retrospective and only applications for the Habitat Scheme, the Nitrate Sensitive Areas scheme or the Woodland Grant Scheme/Farm Woodland Premium Scheme made after the Regulation came into force are eligible. Commission implementing rules concerned primarily with eligibility conditions were subsequently adopted at the Cereals Management Committee.

9.12   In order to take advantage of these provisions the land must be eligible for payments under the Arable Area Scheme and must also meet the normal rules for set-aside.

1995/96 CAP Price Fixing

9.13   At the June Agriculture Council, agreement was reached on the Commission's annual price proposals. This was a relatively uncontroversial package of measures, as price changes for many commodities were already established in the legislation stemming from the 1992 CAP Reform agreement. The main points of the agreed package are described in more detail in the Annex to this Chapter.

Sheepmeat

9.14   On 29-30 May, the Agriculture Council agreed two regulations resulting from the 1994 price fixing settlement: one exempted transfers of quota between producer group members from the 15 per cent "siphon" deduction and also provided for the allocation of an extra 600,000 (maximum) quota rights to each of Greece and Italy because 1991 - the base year for quota allocations - had been a transitional year between two systems; the other extended a derogation applicable in Spain and Portugal to lambs fattened as heavy carcases.

Fresh Meat

9.15   At the June Agriculture Council, agreement was reached on amendments to Directive 64/433/EEC on health conditions for the production and marketing of fresh meat. The main features will make permanent the low throughput limits of 20 livestock units per week for slaughterhouses and 5 tonnes for cutting premises; redefine the number of animals which constitute a "livestock unit" in relation to their weight; allow member states to permit low throughput slaughterhouses to exceed the limits in particular circumstances; and, in exceptional circumstances, extend the temporary derogation from the structural requirements beyond 31 December 1995.   These amendments should be particularly helpful to small premises by providing them with further flexibility.

9.16   The June Agriculture Council also adopted a proposal for a Council decision laying down rules for the microbiological testing by sampling of fresh beef, veal and pigmeat intended for Finland and Sweden. A similar proposal was adopted for the testing of fresh poultrymeat. The decisions, which set out the sampling technique and frequency and lay down the microbiological method for the examination of samples, effectively transfer the requirement to test the meat at the place of origin.

Financing of Veterinary Inspections of Animal Products from Third Countries

9.17   At the June Agriculture Council, a directive was adopted delaying, until 31 December 1996, the application of the standard fee of 5 ecu (£5.94) per tonne in respect of veterinary checks under Directive 90/675/EEC on fresh meat imported from countries which have entered into discussions aimed at establishing veterinary equivalency agreements with the Community. The agreements are intended, among other things, to provide a basis for setting alternative levels of fee to apply to imports of animal products from the countries concerned.

Transitional Arrangements For The Establishment of a Provisional List of Third Country Premises Approved to Export Certain Animal Products to the Community

9.18   The June Agriculture Council adopted a decision detailing provisional measures for the establishment of approved lists of third country premises for a range of animal products. The decision will enable the finalisation of harmonised import rules for those products of animal origin and fish products where, currently, only partial harmonised animal and public health import rules are in place.

9.19   Competent authorities of the approved third countries nominate premises which comply with the Community's import requirements for inclusion on the approved lists. Subsequent adoption is subject to agreement by the Standing Veterinary Committee. As a general rule, nominated premises must, among other things, have been subject to a previous satisfactory inspection visit, either by the Commission or a member state. These provisional measures will apply until 31 December 1996.

Animal Health

9.20   At the June Agriculture Council, a decision was agreed which allows knackers yards to continue to operate, subject to certain standards being met, after 31 December 1995. This is the date on which the derogation exempting knackers yards from the provisions of the Animal Waste Directive 90/667/EEC expires. The decision comes into force on 1 January 1996 and will be reviewed by 31 December 1998. The UK is currently considering how the decision will be implemented.

Fish Health Measures

9.21   The June Agriculture Council adopted a directive amending Directive 91/67/EEC concerning the placing on the market of aquaculture animals and products. This directive defines more clearly the fish health conditions individual fish farms need to meet in order to obtain Community recognition as free from the two most serious diseases of fish currently present in parts of the Community. The directive also clarifies the definition, contained in

Directive 91/67/EEC, of an approved disease-free zone and sets out procedures for the approval, suspension and withdrawal of such zones.

Sugar

9.22   On 10-11 April, the Agriculture Council reached agreement on amendments to the sugar regime which do little more than the minimum necessary to modify the regime to enable the Community's GATT obligations to be met. The main modification enables quota levels to be reduced annually, if necessary, to meet the GATT limits on subsidised exports. There are also provisions to improve the provision of supplies of imported raw cane sugar to refiners. The revised arrangements will operate until 2001.

Rum

9.23   On 6 March, the Council agreed to changes to the quota arrangements by which African, Caribbean and Pacific (ACP) rum is imported into the Community. From 1 January 1996, the quota on light rum will be abolished. A new quota on dark/traditional rum will be introduced from this date which will be increased annually until it is abolished from 1 January 2000. At this point, all rum of ACP origin will enter the Community market duty-free. The Council also agreed to reserve the reduced excise rate which currently benefits all rum sold in France, to rum produced solely within the French Overseas Departments.

Industrial Oilseeds

9.24   In March, the Commission produced a report on the use of oilseeds for non-food purposes and the corrective action which the Community is required to take under its Memorandum of Understanding with the United States, should the by-products from oilseeds for non-food use grown on set-aside land exceed one million tonnes per annum, expressed as soya bean meal equivalents. The Commission is expected to issue a proposal relating to the corrective action later in 1995. In the meantime, a system to monitor quantities of by-products was to be introduced.

FISHERIES

Internal Regime

9.25   On 31 March, following delayed discussions with Norway on shared stocks, the Council agreed amendments to the Regulation on fishing opportunities for 1995.

9.26   On 15 June, the Fisheries Council adopted a regulation implementing the provisions of Article 3 of Council Regulation

685/95/EC by establishing a system of management of fishing effort in western waters. Regulation 685/95/EC provides for the integration of Spain and Portugal into the Common Fisheries Policy from 1 January 1996 and was agreed on 22 December 1994. The new agreement sets effort ceilings for each fishery calculated on the basis of actual effort in 1993 or 1994. Provision is made for adjustments to be made to the levels set to take account of quota swaps or if the levels set prejudice the full use of a member state's quotas. In practice, for the UK fleet, the levels set will allow current fishing activities to continue unchanged, provided effort does not increase.

9.27   At the same meeting, most member states also indicated they could agree to a Presidency compromise concerning a proposal for funds from the existing Financial Instrument for Fisheries Guidance (FIFG) to be used to support national early retirement schemes for fishermen and for compensation payments to crews of decommissioned vessels. The Commission's original proposals relating to bad weather payments and additional support for market price fluctuation were excluded. The UK continued to argue that such measures should be covered by national social policies and were not an appropriate use of FIFG funds. The measures will now be considered by the European Parliament before final decisions are taken.

External Regime

9.28   A dispute with Canada arose in February when the Community objected to a proposal in the North-West Atlantic Fisheries Organisation (NAFO), for allocating, between Contracting Parties, the Total Allowable Catch (TAC) for Greenland halibut in NAFO waters. The proposed allocation would have given significantly increased catch levels to Canada and other non-EU countries, while the Community would have been required to reduce its activity by more than 90 percent. This dispute escalated following Canadian seizure of the Spanish fishing vessel "Estai" in international waters. After intensive negotiations between the Commission and Canada, agreement was reached in April dividing the Canadian and Community quotas approximately evenly between the two sides and introducing a tough new enforcement regime to ensure compliance with fisheries conservation resources in NAFO waters.

Annex to Chapter 9

The Common Agricultural Policy (CAP) Price Settlement for 1995/96 and Related Measures

Cereals And Rice

1.   *There were no price changes beyond the 1992 CAP Reform decisions. Monthly increments were reduced to 1.3 ecu/tonne/month (a reduction of about 10 per cent). An aid of 138.86 ecu per hectare of durum wheat is to be granted, outside traditional regions, in those areas of Austria where there is a well-established production, up to a limit of 5,000 hectares. The Council asked the Commission to examine whether a world price mechanism for protein crops and linseed would safeguard the balance between arable crops. Monthly increments for rice were reduced by 2.5 per cent (2.28 ecu per tonne). The rules for the measurement of grains were amended.*

Sugar

2.   *Support prices were frozen at 1994/95 levels, with the storage refund (paid to offset the cost of private storage) reduced to 4.5 ecu/tonne/month (from 4.8 ecu/tonne/month), to reflect lower interest rates within the Community.*

Olive Oil

3.   *Institutional prices and aid rates remain unchanged for 1995/96. Transitional arrangements for Spain and Portugal were completed by a final adjustment to their production aid, to bring it into line with the rest of the Community.*

4.   *The olive oil regime is due to be reviewed. However, the Commission did not propose changes to the regime at this price fixing since it wished first to study the effects of the decision in 1994 to alter the balance between production aid and consumption aid.*

Dried Fodder

5.   *There were no changes in the price fixing itself, but a separate amending regulation agreed outside the price fixing package increased the size of advance payments.*

Protein Crops and Linseed

6.   *In June, the Council asked the Commission to investigate introducing a mechanism for adjusting area payments, in relation to market prices, for protein crops (peas, field beans and sweet lupins) and linseed, similar to that which exists for oilseeds, to better safeguard the balance between arable crops.*

Cotton

7.   *Reform proposals were agreed by the Council. The separate aid scheme for small producers, which had been abused by large producers dividing their holdings so as to benefit from it, was abolished. Also abolished was the "butoir" system, which had limited the extent to which overproduction could trigger reductions in aid.*

8.   *The guide price was set at 106.3 ecu (£89.50)/100kg and the Maximum Guaranteed Quantity (MGQ) at 1.031 million tonnes, split into national limits between the two main producer member states (Spain and Greece). Reductions in aid will be applied according to overproduction in each state.*

9.   *The Council agreed that the MGQ could be increased to a maximum of 1.120 million tonnes in any year provided that world market prices for cotton were such that this could be done without additional cost to the aid regime.*

10.   *Anti-fraud controls were strengthened, in particular to establish a clearer link between the areas used to grow cotton and the quantities delivered to the processor.*

Wine

11.   *The main aim of the proposals was to extend a number of provisions pending a major reform of the wine regime. These were extension of:*

- *deadlines for reports on wine-growing zones; enrichment; the effects of structural measures and their link with compulsory distillation; and maximum sulphur dioxide levels in wine;*

- *the Dublin compromise rules for calculating distillation quantities;*

- *deacidification practices and aid for grape must for promotion of grape juice;*

- *the derogation provided in the Spanish Accession Act permitting 'coupage' (blending) and lower acidity levels;*

- *the EAGGF funding (50 per cent) for the establishment of vineyard registers, with those member states who had not completed their registers by 1 July 1995 required to establish 'reference chart' by end-1996.*

12.   *Growers may not apply for grants for grubbing areas for which they have received aid for restructuring.*

Fruit and Vegetables

13.   No change in basic prices pending reform of the fruit and vegetables regime. Derogations agreed for citrus processing regulation allowing aid to be paid direct to producers rather than through the processor.

Tobacco

14.   Production premia frozen at 1994/95 levels. Minor changes made to the varietal allocations of certain member states within overall Maximum Guaranteed Quantities.

15.   As envisaged in the 1994/95 price fixing negotiations, the regime has been modified to provide for the allocation of production quotas and the payment of production premium directly to growers (rather than to processors), and the possibility of carrying forward up to 10 per cent of their varietal quotas to the following marketing year.

Seeds

16.   Rates of seed production aid (SPA) for all eligible species were maintained at the same levels for the 1996/97 and 1997/98 marketing years.

Milk

17.   The intervention process for butter and skimmed milk powder were left unchanged, as was the target price for milk. A minimum protein standard was established for skimmed milk powder taken into intervention. From 1 March 1996, the full intervention price will be payable on powder with a minimum protein content of 35.6 per cent of the non-fat dry matter, with a price reduction of 1.75 per cent for each percentage point by which the protein content falls below the minimum standard, down to a level of 31.4 per cent of the non-fat dry matter. Below that level, intervention will not be available.

18.   The Agriculture Council had already agreed in the 1994/95 price settlement that there should be no reduction in milk quotas in 1995/96. The Council accepted a proposal by the Commission that additional milk quota for Italy and Greece, which had been granted provisionally for 1994/95, should be confirmed on a permanent basis for 1995/96 and subsequent years. The Agriculture Council on 29-30 May adopted, in accordance with an agreement reached at ECOFIN in October 1994, a regulation, backdating to 1991/92 and 1992/93, the additional quota which had been awarded to Spain, Italy and Greece in 1993/94 and 1994/95.

Beef

19.   The intervention price was reduced by a further 5 per cent from the beginning of the marketing year, as agreed in the 1992 CAP reform package. The requirement to fix a guide price ended with the

implementation of the GATT agreement and the abolition of variable import levies on 1 July.

20.   *The Commission undertook to authorise the payment of advances of 1995 Beef Special Premium from 16 October 1995, at a rate of 80 per cent.*

Pigmeat

21.   *The basic price was reduced from 1569.76 ecu (£1322)/tonne to 1509.39 (£1271) ecu/tonne. The standard carcass to which the basic price refers changed from "U" grade (50 per cent - 55 per cent lean meat) to "E" grade (55 per cent - 60 per cent lean meat).*

Other

Fisheries

22.   *Following UK pressure, the Commission produced a report on the implications for the marine eco-system of fishing and industrial fishing, in particular. This was communicated to the Fisheries Council on 8 May, for future discussion.*

23.   *On 22 May, the Council agreed new rules which clarify the restrictions on the maximum permitted engine power allowed to beam trawlers when fishing within 12 miles of the coasts of the UK and the Republic of Ireland or in the "plaice box" off the coasts of Denmark, the Federal Republic of Germany and the Netherlands.*

10. Social Affairs

Employment Issues

10.1 The Commission launched its new Social Action Programme for 1995-1997 on 12 April. The Programme was discussed over lunch at the Social Affairs Council on 29 June, but no formal conclusions were drawn.

10.2 In June, the Employment Department and H M Treasury jointly published "Policies and Programmes for Employment in the UK", in response to the Essen European Council's request in December 1994 that member states should draw up "multi-annual programmes" explaining how they are tackling unemployment in five key areas. An interim report on follow-up to the Essen Council's Conclusions on employment, prepared by an ad hoc group of Directors General for Employment, was sent to the Cannes European Council in June together with two Economic Policy Committee reports (on "Progress on Employment Policies in Member States" and "Tax/Benefit Systems' Interaction With Employment").

10.3 On 29 June, the Social Affairs Council adopted an amendment to the Regulation setting up the European Health and Safety Agency in Bilbao, Spain, allowing the launch of the Agency to proceed. The Council also reached political agreement on a common position on a draft directive amending Directive 89/655 on the Use of Work Equipment. Formal adoption of the common position is expected in July without further discussion.

10.4 On 27 March, the Social Affairs Council adopted a Resolution on the Balanced Participation of Men and Women in Decision Making, and one on Improving the Transposition and Implementation of Community Social Legislation.

10.5 On 29 June, the Social Affairs Council adopted a Resolution on the Employment of Older Workers. The Resolution refers to the organisation of work, pay and income, approaches to retirement and training of older workers.

10.6 Conclusions on the Quality of Training were also agreed. The Conclusions note the importance of high quality vocational training and member states' different approaches to improving quality.

10.7   The LEONARDO training programme was launched in Tours on 2-3 March and in London on 4 May. The programme will run for five years and will promote a range of projects and activities involving partnerships between training organisations in different member states.

Education

10.8   On 14 March, the Council and the European Parliament adopted a Decision establishing the SOCRATES programme in the field of education.

10.9   On 31 March, the Education Council adopted a Resolution on Improving and Diversifying Language Learning and Teaching within the Education Systems of the European Union.

10.10 The Council also reached political agreement on a Common Position on the Commission Proposal to make 1996 the European Year of Lifelong Learning.

European Medicines Evaluation Agency

The European Medicines Evaluation Agency (EMEA) was established under Title 4, Article 49, of Council Regulation (EEC) 2309/93, as part of the EC "future systems" package for medicines licensing.

The EMEA, which is based in London and officially came into being on 1 January, was established to take forward the harmonisation of the licensing of medicinal products for human use in the EU required by the "future systems" arrangements for pharmaceutical licensing. The EMEA's responsibilities include overall co-ordination of EC medicines licensing in relation to the new procedures, organisation of assessments for high-technology products which fall under the new centralised procedure and acting as headquarters and secretariat for the EC's Committee for Proprietary Medicinal Products (CPMP) and the Committee for Veterinary Medicinal Products (CVMP).

The Executive Director of the EMEA is Fernand Sauer, a Frenchman, who was formerly head of the European Commission's Pharmaceuticals Unit. The EMEA's Management Board consists of two representatives from each member state.

The decision to site the EMEA in London followed a strong campaign to attract the Agency and is a success story for the UK.

Youth

10.11 On 14 March, the Youth Council and the European Parliament adopted the Decision on the third phase of the Youth for Europe programme. On 31 March, the Youth Council approved, without amendment, the Resolution on Co-operation in the field of Youth Information.

Culture

10.12 At the 3-4 April Culture Council two Presidency Resolutions on Multimedia and the Heritage and Central and Eastern Europe were adopted.

10.13 At the 21 June Council political agreement was reached on a common position on Kaleidoscope and Ministers reached agreement on two decisions to implement the European Community's MEDIA II Programme, which is aimed at developing the European audiovisual industry. MEDIA II will follow the work of the current MEDIA Programme, which is due to end on 31 December 1995. Ministers agreed a total budget for the new programme of 310 million ecu (£165 million) over a five year period: 1 January 1996 to 31 December 2000. MEDIA II will concentrate its support for the European film and television industry around three strategic priority areas: training for professionals and the development and distribution of audiovisual works. The decisions for its implementation are based on two Articles of the Maastricht Treaty, Article 127 (action in the training field) and Article 130 (initiatives to support development and distribution).

Tourism

10.14 The Commission published a Green Paper on the role of the Union in the field of tourism, to which it sought response by 30 June. The Green Paper outlines the history of Community involvement in this area, and goes on to suggest possible options for the level of future activity.

11. Transport

Road Transport

11.1   On 13-14 March, the Transport Council adopted a Resolution on the social harmonisation of road goods transport and agreed a mandate to enable the Commission to open land transport negotiations between the Community and Switzerland. On 19-20 June, the Transport Council adopted a directive establishing uniform procedures for checking vehicles carrying dangerous goods and reached a common position on a directive requiring land transport undertakings to appoint a qualified dangerous goods adviser.

Rail Transport

11.2   On 19-20 June, the Transport Council adopted directives on the licensing of railway undertakings and the allocation of rail infrastructure capacity. The former will establish a Community operating licence that will ensure the application of common conditions of competence for entry into the Community international rail market. The latter will require operators to pay in full the real costs of the facilities that they use and infrastructure managers to cover the full cost of the system. The Transport Council also reached political agreement on a common position on a directive on the interoperability of high-speed trains.

Air Transport

11.3   On 13-14 March, the Transport Council agreed a mandate to enable the Commission to open air transport negotiations between the Community and Switzerland.

11.4   On 26 April, the Commission adopted a proposal for a mandate for Community negotiations to liberalise air services between the Community and the US. On 19-20 June, the Transport Council invited the Commission to undertake a thorough analysis of Community-level negotiations with the US to determine whether such negotiations could produce a better result for all member states than negotiations by member states and also to define the common interest.

11.5   At the request of the UK, the revised traffic distribution rules issued by the French government for the Paris airports system in November 1994 were investigated by the Commission. The Commission's decision of 14 March (to be implemented from the summer of 1996) went a long way toward addressing the practical difficulties of access to Orly airport by redefining the word "route" so that it would apply to traffic between airports rather than airport systems. The French government made further changes to the rules, which now allow for smaller aircraft to be used on services to Orly at peak hours, in May.

Maritime Transport

11.6   In April, the Commission adopted Regulation (EC) 870/95 granting shipping consortia a block exemption, subject to certain conditions, from the competition rules of the Treaty.

11.7   On 19-20 June, the Transport Council adopted Directive 95/21 on port state control. The directive aims to improve maritime safety and pollution prevention in Community waters by codifying and strengthening existing international agreements and will require member states to inspect at least 25 per cent of the foreign ships calling at their ports each year.

Research

11.8   On 1 June, the Commission announced the formation of six research task forces with the stated aim of assisting in the coordination of national and Community research programmes to stimulate the development of technologies to improve the quality of life and industrial competitiveness. Four of the task forces are related to transport: the car of tomorrow; new generation aircraft, the train of tomorrow and intermodality in transport. See also Chapter 15.

11.9   On 19-20 June, the Transport Council agreed conclusions on research in transport. The Council welcomed the plans for transport research in the Fourth Framework Programme and instructed the Commission to explore ways of funding research demonstration projects and to report back to the Council.

12. Structural actions and trans-European Networks

STRUCTURAL FUNDS

Single Programming Documents (SPDs)

12.1   The remaining Objective 5(b) SPDs, which set out the actions to be co-financed in Great Britain under this Objective of the Structural Funds, were approved by the Commission. All SPDs under Objectives 1,2 and 5(b) have now been approved.

Community Initiatives

12.2   In April, the Commission announced allocations totalling 420 million ecu (£354 million) for Community Initiatives to the three new member states, for the period 1995 - 1999, bringing the total allocated funding for the EU-l5 to 12.23 billion ecu (£10.3 billion). The United Kingdom's share of the allocations will be 1150 million ecu (£968 million). There is a reserve of 1.6 billion ecu (£1.35 billion).

12.3   The UK will benefit from all the Initiatives except for REGIS II, for the most remote regions of the EU. The UK sent to the Commission 37 programmes covering the 12 Initiatives for which it is eligible. The Commission has approved a further seven programmes, bringing the total of adopted programmes to nine. Further approvals are expected during the summer.

12.4   The UK PESCA programme was approved on 20 June. The allocation for the programme is 37.43 million ecu (£31.5 million). The initiative is aimed principally at fishery dependent areas and will support projects which contribute to economic diversification and job creation.

12.5   The Great Britain and Northern Ireland programmes for ADAPT were agreed with the Commission on 18 May. The initiative is aimed at assisting the adaptation of the workforce to industrial change and in both programmes the main focus will be employees threatened with redundancy in small and medium sized enterprises. Projects must be transnational and innovative. The UK allocation for ADAPT is 283.5 million ecu (£238.7 million) over the 1995-1999 period.

12.6   The Welsh and Northern Ireland programmes for LEADER II were approved on 29 March. The allocations for these programmes are 8.61 million ecu (£7.17 million) and 11.35 million ecu (£9.45 million) respectively. The initiative is aimed at stimulating rural development and will assist rural associations and other local bodies to promote innovation in rural areas. The programmes will run from 1994-1999.

12.7   The Norther Ireland URBAN programme was approved on 27 February. Its aim is to regenerate depressed urban areas by encouraging economic and social revitalisation, improving infrastructure and promoting environmental improvements. The allocation for the programme is 16.95 million ecu (£14.12 million) over the period 1994-1999.

12.8   The Northern Ireland SME programme was approved on 28 March. The main focus of the initiative is "to stimulate small and medium-sized industrial or service enterprises, particularly in the less developed regions, to adapt to the Single Market, and to ensure that they become internationally competitive". The programme will run from 1994-1999 with an allocation of 6.2 million ecu (£5.16 million).

Northern Ireland

12.9   The Special Support Programme for Peace and Reconciliation for Northern Ireland and the border counties of the Republic of Ireland was agreed with the Commission on 28 July. The programme aims to reinforce progress towards a peaceful and stable society and to promote reconciliation by increasing economic development and employment, promoting urban and rural regeneration, developing cross-border co-operation and extending social inclusion. Of the £240 million Community funding allocated to the Programme, an indicative amount of £190 million has been allocated to Northern Ireland across a total of 8 Sub-programmes. The allocation is in respect of the years 1995-1997 and further funding may be available for an additional 2 years depending on the outcome of the review of the Programme.

International Fund for Ireland

12.10 The Fund received a contribution of 3 million ecu (£2.5 million) which is the final tranche for 1994. The European Community confirmed an increase in its pledge to the Fund from 15 million ecu (£12.6 million) per year to 20 million ecu (£16.8 million) per year for the period 1995-97. It is Fund policy that three quarters of its disbursements are spent in Northern Ireland.

TRANS-EUROPEAN NETWORKS (TENS)

Community Financial Aid

12.11 The Commission issued a revised proposal for a Council regulation laying down general rules for the procedure for the granting of Community financial aid in the field of Trans-European Networks on 17 March, taking into account the European Parliament's amendments to the original proposal. The Council reached a common position on the proposed regulation on 31 March.

Transport

12.12 On 19-20 June, the Transport Council adopted a common position on the proposal for a decision identifying guidelines for transport TENs which will establish eligible projects ("projects of common interest" (PCIs)).

Energy

12.13 On 29 June, the Council adopted a common position on both the guidelines and the favourable context Decisions. The first covers the objectives and priorities to which TENs will contribute and sets out broad lines of action, including the identification of PCIs. The second is one of the broad lines of action identified and provides for technical co-operation between those responsible for TENs and the promotion of co-operation between member states to facilitate the implementation of authorisation procedures. It also enables the Commission to provide financial assistance for feasibility studies for PCIs and studies aimed at improving technical co-operation.

Telecommunications

12.14 The Commission issued a proposal for a European Parliament and Council decision on guidelines for trans-European telecommunications networks on 31 May.

Cannes European Council

12.15 The Cannes European Council on 26-27 June welcomed the progress of the priority projects endorsed by the Essen European Council. It called on the Commission to seek out any other possible means of funding to speed up the implementation of projects. Finally, it agreed that the fourteen transport priority projects would represent 75 per cent of the appropriations available under the "networks" heading in 1995 and 1996.

13. Industrial, Consumer and Energy Issues

Competitiveness

13.1   On 7 April, the Industry Council reached conclusions on industrial competitiveness, which were broadly in line with UK thinking, as set out in the White Paper "Forging Ahead". In February, the Commission established a high-level Competitiveness Advisory Group under the chairmanship of Dr Ciampi "to advise on the major policy priorities that must be carried out in order to improve the European Union's competitiveness". It produced its first report in time for the Cannes European Council, which noted the report with satisfaction.

Competition: Renewal of Cars Block Exemption

13.2   On 29 June, the Commission published EC Regulation 1475/95 governing the distribution and servicing of cars in the EU. This will replace EC Regulation 123/85 with effect from 1 October 1995. While the new regulation maintains the basic elements of selective and exclusive distribution, dealers will have greater freedom to sell competing brands and to advertise outside their contract areas. Consumers will benefit from increased choice and competition between brands.

Competition: EC/US Agreement

13.3   On 10 April, the Council and the Commission approved the agreement between the European Communities and the Government of the United States regarding the application of their competition laws, including an exchange of interpretative letters.

Telecommunications

13.4   On 13 June, the Telecommunications Council agreed a Resolution on a future regulatory framework for telecommunications, necessary to implement the full liberalisation of network infrastructure and services by 1 January 1998. A Resolution arising from the outcome of the Commission's consultation on its Green Paper on policy in the mobile and personal communications sector was also agreed. The Council also agreed a common position on the resubmitted directive applying Open Network Provision to voice telephony. The Council also agreed conclusions on a draft Commission directive on the use of cable television networks for the provision of telecoms services already liberalised by the Community.

Small and Medium-Sized Enterprises (SMEs)

13.5   The Council considered a Commission strategy paper for SMEs. It called upon the Commission to submit a report to it on current policies and on ways of improving their effectiveness through measures, particularly of a fiscal nature, aimed at promoting the creation of SMEs, reducing the administrative burdens on them and facilitating their participation in training and research programmes. The Commission will present its report to the Madrid European Council in December 1995.

13.6   The Government endorses the need for a clear strategy for Community SME policy. It stresses that primary responsibility in this area rests with member states. Action at Community level should concentrate on issues that member states cannot address better themselves. Future strategy should also take account of current Community policies, for example under the SME multiannual programme, which is due to finish at the end of 1996. A Commission report evaluating that programme will issue in March 1996, after which final decisions about future strategy will be taken.

Energy Policy

13.7   Following consultations with member states and pan-European industry bodies, the Commission produced a Green Paper entitled 'For a European Union Energy Policy'. On 1 June, the Energy Council adopted a Resolution on the Green Paper acknowledging the Community's existing energy policy and the on-going work towards the completion of the internal energy market. The Resolution touched on most areas of energy policy including security of supply, competitiveness, and energy and the environment. It broadly confirmed that the Commission should continue in its current role including regular assessment of existing legislation. The Resolution is intended to give a steer to the Commission in its formulation of the White Paper which is expected later this year.

Internal Energy Market

13.8   On 1 June, the Energy Council agreed conclusions noting that the two systems of negotiated Third Party Access and the Single Buyer could co-exist subject to conditions to secure reciprocity and equivalence between the two systems. Although agreement had been reached on a number of conditions, notably the need for authorisation of independent power producers outside the tendering procedures, a number of issues still remain to be resolved. Furthermore, the Commission has produced a working paper on small and very small systems, as requested by the Council. The objective is to reach a common position by the end of 1995.

Energy Charter Treaty

13.9   The Energy Charter Treaty closed for signature on 16 June. All negotiating parties signed the Treaty except the US and Canada. The Treaty is the first:

- major economic agreement between the Former Soviet Union and the West;

- international agreement enshrining free trade in energy products in international law;

- multilateral agreement covering investment and trade;

- agreement to elaborate rules of transit.

13.10 Negotiations on a second Treaty to enshrine the means of applying national treatment for the admission of investments have begun and are expected to be concluded in 1998.

14. Environment

Control of Major Accident Hazards involving Dangerous Substances

14.1   On 22-23 June, the Environment Council reached a common position on the proposal for a new directive on major accident hazards. The directive closely follows UK philosophy and practice and is intended to update the existing "Seveso" Directive (82/501), adopted in the wake of various industrial accidents. The new directive introduces revisions based on ten years' experience.

Regulation on Trade in Endangered Species

14.2   On 22-23 June, the Environment Council reached political agreement on a new regulation to replace the existing CITES (Convention on International Trade in Endangered Species) measure. The UK welcomed the new regulation which will require member states to control trade in endangered species more effectively. The Council also agreed to a UK proposal to retain the existing 1981 regulation banning commercial imports of whale products.

Integrated Pollution Prevention and Control

On 22-23 June, the Environment Council reached a common position on a Directive on Integrated Pollution Prevention and Control (IPPC). The directive applies to the largest, most polluting plants and requires them to be issued with permits, based on best available techniques, to achieve a high level of protection for the environment as a whole. The directive mirrors the approach followed in the UK since 1990, when the Environment Protection Act introduced integrated pollution control.

The directive requires a fully coordinated approach to the setting of emission limits to air, water and land. It aims to encourage the development of clean technologies to achieve overall environmental benefits, and is a radical and major step forward from the "end of pipe" approach and single medium regulation. The directive will begin making a real impact, improving the environmental performance of new plants coming on stream before the end of the century, as well as existing ones which are undergoing substantial modifications. It also applies to all existing plants whose performance will be improved to a demanding timetable. Overall, the directive will raise environmental standards across Europe and help to provide a level playing field for British industry.

The directive is due to come into force three years after its publication. A transition period of eight years is envisaged for existing plant.

Air Quality Framework Directive

14.3   On 22-23 June, the Environment Council agreed a common position on the Air Quality Framework Directive, designed to provide a strategic framework to tackle air pollution across Europe. The directive closely reflects the UK's air quality strategy and complements the Government's domestic proposals for an air quality strategy.

14.4   The directive will set mandatory limit values for pollutants which member states will have to attain within a specified time period. It will also set alert thresholds at levels where short-term exposure to pollutant levels might pose a threat to human health. It also contains guidelines for minimum levels of pollutant monitoring. Member states will be obliged to produce plans showing the measures to be taken if limit values are exceeded. These plans could include traffic restrictions and other controls.

14.5   The directive sets the pattern for further proposals to reduce the levels of thirteen major pollutants. These further proposals will set numerical goals for the standards this directive establishes. The first of these, SO2, NO2, fine particles, suspended particle materials and lead, are due to be submitted by the Commission by the end of 1996. By the end of 1999, proposals are due on benzene, polycyclic aromatic hydrocarbons, carbon monoxide, cadmium, arsenic, nickel and mercury.

14.6   On ozone, proposals are due before 1 March 1998, in line with Directive 92/72, and have to take account of the specific mechanisms for ozone formation. To this end, provision may be made for target values and/or limit values. The UK made a declaration at the Council that it may be necessary to fix a guide value not only for ozone but also for other secondary transfrontier pollutants such as photochemical particles.

14.7   The UK urged other member states to act quickly to tackle ozone pollution by limiting emissions of its precursors and called on the Commission to bring forward proposals for ozone as quickly as possible.

Climate Change

14.8   The European Union played a leading part in the Berlin Conference of the Parties to the Climate Change Convention, held in March-April 1995. The Conference agreed a mandate for the preparation of a protocol to set out an approach combining policies, measures, targets and timetables for reducing emissions of greenhouse gases in the period after the year 2000.

14.9 On 22-23 June, the Environment Council agreed Conclusions on the follow-up to the Conference. The Council welcomed the decision to strengthen commitments for the period after the year 2000 and invited the Commission to notify it as soon as possible of projected greenhouse gas emissions up to 2000 and to draw up a proposal for emissions to be monitored after that date. The Council asked member states to report on the steps they intended to take and the objectives they proposed to achieve for 2005 and 2010, and called for the Commission to put forward proposals for reducing CO2 emissions from vehicles and for reducing other greenhouse gases.

Basel Convention on the Control of Transboundary Movements of Hazardous Wastes and their Disposal

14.10 On 9 March, the Environment Council agreed that the Community should submit a proposal for the amendment of the Basel Convention, with a view to its adoption at the third Conference of the Parties. The amendment, reflecting a decision already taken by the second Conference of the Parties, would allow the parties to prohibit any transboundary movement of hazardous wastes for final disposal from OECD member countries to countries which are not OECD members. On 22-23 June, the Environment Council agreed that the amendment should reflect the full scope of the decision taken at the second Conference, and should therefore relate also to a ban on the movement of hazardous wastes for recovery from OECD to non-OECD countries. The Council gave the Commission a negotiating mandate for the Conference to this effect. Separately, the Commission submitted a proposal to reflect the amendment in Regulation 259/93, which implements the Basel Convention in the Community.

15. Research and Development

Fourth European Community Framework Programme for Research and Development (FP4): Task Forces

15.1   At the 10 March Research Council, Commissioner Cresson outlined Commission plans to establish industry/research Task Forces. The Task Forces would aim to reinforce the European Union's capacity to transform research and development into industrial and commercial success by re-grouping and concentrating EU resources. Initially five specific areas were envisaged: the car of tomorrow, multimedia educational software, new generation aircraft, viral vaccines and diseases and the train of the future. When the Task Forces were officially announced on 1 June, a sixth Task Force, on intermodality in transport, was added.

Co-ordination of Research

15.2   At its 9 June meeting the Research Council adopted a Commission paper on Co-ordination of European research policies. The conclusions provided for the creation of ad hoc committees in the different areas covered by FP4 to analyse topics on which closer co-operation between Community and national programmes might be worthwhile.

16. Parliamentary Scrutiny of EC Legislation

16.1   348 documents were deposited in Parliament. In addition 81 unnumbered explanatory memoranda were submitted where a depositable document was not available or had not been received.

16.2   The diagrams below provide details of how the House of Commons Select Committee on European Legislation and the House of Lords Select Committee on the European Communities reported on documents considered during the period 1 January - 30 June.

16.3   22 debates on European Community documents were held in the House of Commons including, one on the Floor of the House, five in European Standing Committee A and 16 in European Standing Committee B. The House of Lords Select Committee on the European Communities published 10 reports, five for information of the House and five for debate. Three reports were debated. Further information about scrutiny debates in both Houses, and reports published by the House of Lords Select Committee can be found in Appendices E and F.

House of Commons	House of Lords

Not Legally or Political Important:
229 documents

For debate:
30 documents

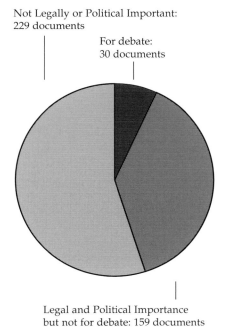

For further consideration in Sub-Committee:
101 documents

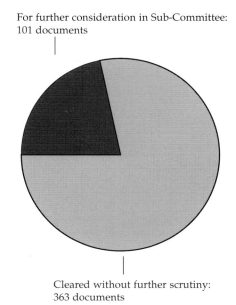

Legal and Political Importance
but not for debate: 159 documents

Cleared without further scrutiny:
363 documents

Appendix A: Major Proposals Adopted

Economic and Budgetary

Council Decision 95/132/EC - providing macro-financial assistance for Belarus. Adopted 10 April. See paragraph 6.16

Council Decision 95/207/EC - granting a Community guarantee to the European Investment Bank against losses under loans for projects in South Africa. Adopted 1 June.

Council Decision 95/250/EC - relating to exceptional Community aid for the reconstruction of the areas stricken by the cyclone that hit Madeira in October 1993. Adopted 29 June.

European Parliament and Council Directive 95/26/EC - (post BCCI Directive) amending Directives 77/780/EEC and 89/646/EEC in the field of credit institutions, Directives 73/239/EEC and 92/49/EEC in the field of non-life insurance, Directives 79/267/EEC and 92/96/EEC in the field of life assurance, Directive 93/22/EEC in the field of investment firms and Directive 85/611/EEC in the field of undertakings for collective investment in transferable securities (UCITS), with a view to reinforcing prudential supervision. Adopted 29 June.

Council Directive 95/7/EC - amending Directive 77/388/EEC and introducing new simplification measures with regard to value added tax - scope of certain exemptions and practical arrangements for implementing them.

Agriculture and Food

Council Regulations on support prices for the 1995/96 marketing year, flowing from Commission Document COM(95)34. Adopted 29 June.

Council Regulation 150/95 - amending Regulation 3813/92/EEC on the unit of account and the conversion rates to be applied for the purposes of the Common Agricultural Policy. Adopted 23 January.

Council Regulation 711/95 - amending Regulation 2075/95/EEC on the common organisation of the market in raw tobacco. Adopted 27 March.

Council Regulation 1101/95 - amending Regulation 1785/81/EEC on the common organisation of the market in the sugar sector and Regulation 1010/86/EEC laying down general rules for the production refund on certain sugar products used in the chemical industry. Adopted 24 April.

Council Regulation 1287/95 - amending Regulation 729/70/EEC on the financing of the Common Agricultural Policy. Adopted 22 May. See paragraph 9.3.

Council Regulation 1265/95 - amending Regulation 3013/89/EEC on the common organisation of the market in sheepmeat and goatmeat. Adopted 29 May.

Council Regulation 1266/95 - amending Regulation 3901/89/EEC defining lambs fattened as heavy carcases. Adopted 29 May. See paragraph 9.13.

Council Regulation 1161/95 - amending the number of further reference periods in the context of the agrimonetary system. Adopted 22 May.

Council Regulation 1288/95 - extending to the periods 1991/92 and 1992/93 the increase adopted for the periods 1993/94 and 1994/95 in the total quantities fixed for Greece, Spain and Italy under the system for the additional levy in the milk and milk products sector. Adopted 29 May.

Council Regulation 1460/95 - amending Regulation 1765/92 establishing a support system for producers of certain arable crops. Adopted 22 June.

Council Regulation 1527/95 - regarding temporary rules for compensation for reductions in prices and payments due to green rate revaluations before 1 January 1996. Adopted 29 June.

Council Regulation 1538/95 - amending Regulation 804/68/EEC on the common organisation of the market in milk and milk products. Adopted 29 June.

Council Regulation 1539/95 - fixing the target price for milk and the intervention prices for butter and skimmed milk powder for the period from 1 July 1995 to 30 June 1996. Adopted 29 June.

Council Regulation 1552/95 - amending Regulation 3950/92/EEC establishing an additional levy in the milk and milk products sector. Adopted 29 June.

Council Regulation 1553/95 - adjusting, for the fifth time, the system of aid for cotton introduced by Protocol 4 annexed to the Act of Accession of Greece. Adopted 29 June.

Council Regulation 1554/95 - laying down the general rules for the system of aid for cotton and repealing Regulation 2169/81/EEC. Adopted 29 June.

Council Regulation 1935/95 - amending Regulation 2092/91 on organic production of agricultural products and indications referring thereto on agricultural products and foodstuffs. Adopted 22 June.

Council Decision 95/409 - laying down the rules for the microbiological testing by sampling of fresh beef and veal and pigmeat intended for Finland and Sweden. Adopted 22 June. See paragraph 9.15.

Council Decision 95/410 - laying down the rules for the microbiological testing by sampling in the establishment of origin of poultry for slaughter intended for Finland and Sweden. Adopted 22 June.

Council Decision 95/411 - laying down the rules for the microbiological testing for salmonella by sampling of fresh poultrymeat intended for Finland and Sweden. Adopted 22 June. See paragraph 9.15.

Council Directive 95/23 - amending Directive 64/433/EEC on conditions for the production and marketing of fresh meat. Adopted 22 June. See paragraph 9.14.

Council Directive 95/24 - amending the Annex to Directive 85/73/EEC on the financing of veterinary inspections and controls of animal products covered by Annex A to Directive 89/662/EEC and by Directive 90/675/EEC. Adopted 22 June. See paragraph 9.15.

Council Directive 95/25/EC - amending Directive 64/432/EEC on health problems affecting intra-Community trade in bovine animals and swine. Adopted 22 June.

Council Directive 95/29/EC - amending Directive 91/628/EEC concerning the protection of animals during transport. Adopted 29 June.

Fisheries

Council Regulation 685/95 - on the management of the fishing effort relating to certain Community fishing areas and resources. Adopted 27 March, on the basis of agreement reached at the Fisheries Council on 22 December 1994. See paragraph 9.25.

Council Regulation 746/95 - amending Regulation 3362/94/EC fixing, for certain fish stocks and groups of fish stocks, the total allowable catches for 1995 and certain conditions under which they may be fished. Adopted 31 March.

Council Regulation 915/95 (amended by Regulation 1404/95 - adopted on 15 June) - opening and providing for the adminstration of autonomous Community tariff quotas for certain fishery products (1995). Adopted 21 April.

Council Regulation 992/95 - opening and providing for the administration of Community tariff quotas for certain agricultural and fishery products originating in Norway. Adopted 10 April.

Council Regulation 1173/95 - amending for the sixteenth time, Regulation 3094/86/EEC laying down certain technical measures for the conservation of fishery resources. Adopted 22 May.

Council Regulation 1299/95 - amending Regulation 3136/95/EC fixing the guide prices for the fishery products listed in Annex I (A), (D), and (E) of Regulation 3759/92/EEC for the 1995 fishing year. Adopted 6 June.

Council Regulation 1300/95 - amending Regulation 104/76/EEC laying down common marketing standards for shrimps (Crangon crangon), edible crabs (Cancer pagurus) and Norway lobsters (Nephrops norvegius). Adopted 6 June.

Council Regulation 2028/95 - establishing a system for the management of fishing effort relating to certain Community fishing areas and resources. Adopted 15 June.

Council Decision 95/408 - on the conditions for drawing up, for an interim period, provisional lists of third country establishments from which member states are authorised to import certain products of animal origin, fishery products or live bivalve molluscs. Adopted 22 June.

Social Affairs

Council Regulation - amending Regulation EC/267/94 on the European Agency for Safety and Health. Adopted 29 June. See paragraph 10.3.Council Regulation EC/297/95 - setting out the level of fees to be charged by the new European Evaluation Agency (EMEA). Adopted 10 February.

Council Decision - on the third phase of the Youth for Europe programme. Adopted 14 March. See paragraph 10.11.

Council Resolution - on the Balanced Participation of Men and Women in Decision-making. Adopted 27 March. See paragraph 10.4.

Council Resolution - on Improving and Diversifying Language Learning and Teaching within the Education Systems of the European Union. Adopted 31 March. See paragraph 10.8.

Council Resolution - on the Transposition and Implementation of Community Social Legislation. Adopted 27 March. See paragraph 10.4.

Council Resolution - on the Employment of Older Workers. Adopted 29 June. See paragraph 10.5.

Transport

European Parliament and Council Directive 95/1/EC - on the maximum design speed, maximum torque and maximum net engine power of two- or three-wheel motor vehicles. Adopted 17 March.

Council Directive 95/21/EC - on the enforcement, in respect of shipping using Community ports and sailing in the waters under the jurisdiciton of the member states, of international standards for ship safety, pollution prevention and shipboard living and working conditions (port state control). Adopted 19-20 June. See paragraph 11.7.

Council Directive - on uniform control procedures for checks on the transport of dangerous goods by road. Adopted 29 June. See paragraph 11.1.

Council Directive - on the allocation of railway infrastructure capacity and the charging of infrastructure fees. Adopted 29 June. See paragraph 11.2.

Council Directive - on the licensing of railway undertakings. Adopted 29 June. See paragraph 11.2.

Environment

European Parliament and Council Directive 95/27/EEC - amending Council Directive 86/662 on the limitation of noise emitted by hydraulic excavators, rope-operated excavators, dozers, loaders and excavator-loaders. Adopted 29 June.

Trade and Industry

Council Resolution - on the future regulatory framework for telecommunications. Adopted 13 June. See paragraph 13.5.

Council Resolution - on further development of mobile and personal communications in the European Union. Adopted 13 June. See paragraph 13.5.

European Parliament and Council Directive - on Lifts. Adopted on 22 June.

European Parliament and Council Directive - on an information exchange procedure on national measures derogating from the free movement of goods. Adopted 29 June.

Appendix B: Major Treaties and Agreements

Community Alone Treaties

Argentina

Agreement in the form of an Exchange of Letters extending the adaptation to the Agreement on Trade in Mutton, Lamb and Goatmeat.
Signed in Brussels, 22 December 1994

Bulgaria

Agreement in the form of an Exchange of Letters extending the adaptation to the Agreement on Trade in Mutton, Lamb and Goatmeat.
Signed in Brussels, 22 December 1994

Agreement on Free Trade and Trade-related Matters between the European Community, the European Atomic Energy Community and the European Coal and Steel Community, of the one part, and the Republic of Bulgaria, of the other part, with the Final Act.
Signed in Brussels, 30 December 1994

Denmark

Agreement in the form of an Exchange of Letters concerning the amendment to the Agreement on Fisheries between the European Economic Community, on the one hand, and the Government of Denmark and the local Government of Greenland, on the other hand.
Signed in Brussels, 19 December 1994

Third Protocol laying down the Condition relating to Fishing provided for in the Agreement on Fisheries between the European Economic Community, on the one hand, and the Government of Denmark and the local Government of Greenland, on the other hand.
Signed in Brussels, 19 December 1994

European Energy Charter

Final Act of the European Energy Charter Conference with Decisions, Energy Charter Treaty and Energy Charter Protocol on Energy Efficiency and Related Environmental Aspects.
Signed in Lisbon, 17 December 1994

Greenland

Agreement in the Form of an Exchange of Letters concerning the amendment to the Agreement on Fisheries between the European Economic Community, on the one hand, and the Government of Denmark and the local Government of Greenland on the other hand.
Signed in Brussels, 19 December 1994

Third Protocol laying down the Condition relating to Fishing provided for in the Agreement on Fisheries between the European Economic Community, on the one hand, and the Government of Denmark and the local Government of Greenland, on the other hand.
Signed in Brussels, 19 December 1994

Hungary
Agreement in the form of an Exchange of Letters extending the Adaptation to the Agreement on Trade in Mutton, Lamb and Goatmeat.
Signed in Brussels, 21 December 1994

India
Agreement in the form of an Exchange of Letters on the Guaranteed Prices for Cane Sugar for 1993/1994.
Signed in Brussels, 7 December 1994

Morocco
Agreement in the form of an Exchange of Letters on the Regime for Imports into the Community of Tomatoes and Courgettes originating in and imported from Morocco.
Signed in Brussels, 22 December 1994

Poland
Agreement in the form of an Exchange of Letters extending the Adaptation to the Agreement on the Trade in Mutton, Lamb and Goatmeat.
Signed in Brussels, 22 December 1994

Slovak Republic
Agreement in the form of an Exchange of Letters extending the Adaptation to the Agreement on Trade in Mutton, Lamb and Goatmeat.
Signed in Brussels, 21 December 1994

Uruguay
Agreement in the form of an Exchange of Letters extending the Adaptation to the Agreement on Trade in Mutton, Lamb and Goatmeat.
Signed in Brussels, 20 December 1994

Appendix C: European Union Declarations and Statements

EU Declarations (* = with associated CEEs)

Date		Topic
6 January		Palestine, Peace process
17 January		Chechnya
20 January		Somalia
23 January		Israel
23 January		Algeria
23 January		Ex-Yugoslavia
23 January		Chechnya
30 January	*	Algeria, NPT
30 January		Sri Lanka
30 January		Afghanistan
1 February		Peru/Eduador
1 February		Algeria, NPT
6 February		Middle East
6 February		Ex-Yugoslavia
6 February	*	Chechnya, Ceasefire
7 February		Niger, Elections
13 February		Indonesia, Pakpahan
13 February		Iran, Rushdie
14 February		Sierra Leone
21 February	*	Angola
28 February	*	Argentinia, NPT
28 February		Pakistan
28 February	*	China
3 March		North Korea
13 March	*	Burma
19 March		Burundi
20 March	*	Kazakhstan
20 March		Sri Lanka
21 March	*	Gambia
22 March	*	Nigeria
1 April		Chechnya
5 April		Turkey
5 April		Cuba
7 April		Kazakhstan
10 April		Palestinian Elections
11 April		Turkey
11 April		Israel, Palestinian Elections
19 April		Samachki
20 April		Oklahoma
21 April		Sri Lanka
24 April		Kibeho
6 May		Croatia
10 May		Niger
12 May		Rwanda

15 May		East Jerusalem (expropriations)
15 May	*	NPT
18 May		Sierra Leone
29 May		Sri Lanka
29 May		Bosnia
2 June		Rwanda
2 June		Ex-Yugoslavia
7 June		China, Human Rights
8 June		Mostar
9 June		Chile
15 June		Colombia
16 June		South Africa (dealth penalty)
23 June		Burundi
25 June		Haiti, Elections
30 June		Nigeria

EU Statements

23 January		Ex-Yugoslavia
30 January		Sri Lanka
30 January		Afghanistan
30 January	*	Algeria, NPT
30 January		Algiers
6 February		Cairo Summit
6 February		Chechnya
6 February		Ex-Yugoslavia
13 February		Rushdie Fatwa
17 February		OMONIA
28 February	*	Argentina, NPT
11 April		Turkey
10 May		Angola
29 May		Sakhalin Earthquake
9 June	*	Chile, NPT
16 June		Budennovsk

Appendix D, Part 1: List of European Court of Justice Cases involving the United Kingdom

This list includes all cases awaiting judgment and those in which judgment was received during the period. An asterisk denotes those cases in which the United Kingdom applied to intervene or submitted Observations/Pleadings during the period.

(i) Actions initiated by the United Kingdom under Article 173 of the EEC Treaty.

1.   C-471/93: United Kingdom -v- Commission (See C-47/94) (joined cases)

2.   C-47/94: United Kingdom -v- Commission (Challenge to Commission decision relating to Milk quota disallowance to Italy, Spain & Greece for 1990).

3.   C-84/94: United Kingdom -v- Council (Concerning the United Kingdom's challenge to the Working Time Directive).

4.   C-150/94: United Kingdom -v- Council (Application seeking the annulment of Council Regulation 519/94 in so far as it imposes quantitative quotas on three categories of toys originating in China).

5.   C-274/94: United Kingdom -v- Commission (Seeking the annulment of Commission Decision C23/94 of 27 July 1994 on the increase capitalization of Air France. Stayed pending decision of CFI in T371/94)(British Airways & Others -v- Commission).

(ii) Direct actions against the United Kingdom under Article 169 of the EEC Treaty.

1.   C-222/94: Commission -v- United Kingdom (Directive 89/552/EEC on the coordination of certain provisions laid down on member states concerning the permit of television broadcasting activities. The Commission allege that the UK has failed to implement this directive correctly).

(iii) Cases referred to the European Court under Article 177 of the EEC Treaty from United Kingdom courts or tribunals.

1.   C-48/93: The Queen -v- Secretary of State for Transport Ex parte : Factortame Ltd and Others. (Concerning Articles 7, 52 and 221 of the EEC Treaty)(Joined cases C46/93 and C48/93).

2.   C-324/93: The Queen -v- The Secretary of State for the Home Department.Interv: Generics (UK) Limited Ex Parte: Evans Medical Limited and Another (On the import of diamorphine into the United Kingdom and Article 30, 36, and 234 of the EEC Treaty. Judgment 28.3.95. See Part 2 of this appendix).

3.   C-327/93: The Queen -v- Secretary of State for National Heritage Ex Parte : Continental

Television BVio and Others (Directive 89/552/EEC and the proscription of Red Hot Television received in the UK directly via satellite from another member state).

4.   C-342/93: Gillespie and Others -v- Various Health Boards and The Department of Health and Social Services (Article 119 of EEC Treaty and Directive 75/117 EEC whether a woman absent from work on maternity leave is entitled to the full pay (including increases) she would have received if at work).

5.   C-392/93: The Queen -v- H.M. Treasury Ex Parte: British Telecommunications plc (Procurement procedures in telecommunications sector - damages).

6.   C-403/93: Mr M.J.C. Evans, the Executors of Mrs P.J. Evans -v- Metropolitan Police Authority (Article 119 EC Treaty Police Pension Regulations 1973: Widower's Pension).

7.   C-440/93: The Queen -v- Licensing Authority of The Department of Health (1) Norgine Limited (2) Ex Parte: Scotia (Failing to comply with Directive 75/318, 75/319 and 65/65 marketing authorization for medicinal products).

8.   C-4/94: BLP Group PLC -v- Commissioners of Customs and Excise (Deductibility of import value added tax payable in respect of services received relating to the disposal of shares. Judgment 6.4.95. See Part 2 of this appendix).

9.   C-5/94: The Queen -v- MAFF (Challenge to MAFF of former policy not to grant international animal transport certificates pursuant to legislation implementing directive 81/839 in respect of exports of live sheep to Spain).

10.   C-13/94: P -v- S and Cornwall County Council (Directive 76/207: Dismissal of a transsexual.)

11.   C-18/94: Barbara Hopkins and Others -v- (1) National Power (2) Powergen PLC (Coal and Steel prices: Article 86 EC Treaty: Articles 4 and 63 (1) ECSC).

12.   C-38/94: The Queen -v- MAFF Ex Parte: Country Landowners Association (Relating to the Sheep Annual Premium and the Suckler Cow Premium quotas.)

13.   C-44/94: The Queen -v- MAFF Ex Parte: National Federation of Fishermen's organisation and Others (Whether Commission Decision 92/593 permits restrictions on the number of days that all British Fishing Vessels over 10 metres in length can spend at Sea).

14.   C-92/94: 1) Secretary of State for Social Security 2) Chief Adjudication Officer -v- Rose Graham and Others (Directive 79/7: invalidity benefits).

15.   C-112/94: Richardson -v- Barnes (Article 119/EC: Compensation for unfair dismissal. Removed from the Register 3.10.94).

16.   C-116/94: Jennifer Meyers -v- Adjudication Officer (Directive 76/207 and whether Family Credit falls within its scope).

17.   C-127/94: The Queen -v- Ministry of Agriculture, Fisheries and Food Ex parte: Ecroyd and Others (Entitlement to milk quota's Pursuant to Regulation (EEC) No 857/84, as amended by Regulation (EEC) No 764/89 and Council Regulation (EEC) No 1639/91).

18.   C-137/94: The Queen -v- Secretary of State for Health Ex-Parte·Cyrill Richardson (Directive 79/7/EEC in relation to prescription charges).

19.   C-153/94: The Queen -v- Commissioners of Customs and Excise Ex-Parte 1) Faroe Seafood Co Ltd and 2) Foroya Fiskasola (Council Regulation 2051/74,Commission Regulation

3184/74, Council Regulation 1697/79 and Commission Regulation 2164/91: post-clearance custom duties joined with C-204/94 below).

20.   C-155/94: The Wellcome Trust Ltd -v- The Commissioners of Customs and Excise (Concerning Article 4 of the Sixth Directive of EC Council).

21.   C-175/94: The Queen -v- Secretary of State For The Home Department Ex Parte: John Gerald Gallagher (Concerning Council Directive 64/221).

22.   C-201/94: The Queen -v- The Medicine Control Agency and Others Ex-Parte: Smith & Nephew and Primecrown. (Concerning free movement of goods and parallel importing and the system of licensing for medicines).

23.   C-204/94: The Queen -v- Commissioners of Customs and Excise Ex-Parte: John and Celia Smith trading as Arthur Smith (a firm) (joined with case C-153/94).

24.   C-212/94: F.M.C. PLC and Others -v- IBAP and MAFF (Concerning clawback of variable slaughter premium upon export of sheep from Great Britain).

25.   C-228/94: Stanley Charles Atkins -v- 1) Wrekin District Council 2) Department of Transport (Directive 79/7/EEC: concessionary fares on public transport).

26.   C-229/94: The Queen -v- Secretary of State for the Home Department - Ex Parte Gerard Adams (Freedom of movement and national security. Removed from the Register 12.4.95).

27.   C-235/94: Alan Geoffrey Bird -v- Vehicle Inspectorate (Regulation 3820/85: Social legislation relating to road transport - drivers hours).

28.   C-237/94: John O'Flyn -v- Adjudication Officer (Regulation 1612/68: funeral expenses-territorial condition).

29.   *C-288/94: Argos Distributors Ltd -v- Commissioners of Customs and Excise (Sixth VAT Directive and "money-off" vouchers).

30.   *C-302/94: R -v- Secretary of State for Trade and Industry - Ex Parte: British Telecommunications Plc (Directive 92/44 on the application of open network provisions to leased lines).

31.   *C-317/94: Elida Gibbs Ltd -v- Commissioners of Customs and Excise (Sixth VAT Directive - "money-off" and "cash-back" coupons).

32.   *C-27/95: Woodspring District Council -v- Bakers of Nailsea (Veterinary inspection fees: Directive 91/497).

(iv) Cases referred to the European Court under Article 177 of the EEC Treaty from other Member States' courts or tribunals in which Observations have been submitted by the United Kingdom.

1.   C-205/90: NV "Les Assurances du Credit" -v- 1) P.V.A.B. and 2) G Decoopman (ATA Convention: Articles 9 & 12 EEC Treaty: 6th VAT Directive).

2.   C-238-240/91: Criminal Proceedings -v- Henryon & Others (Sale of unapproved telephones - Directive 88/301. Removed from the register 1.12.94).

3.	C-288/91: Criminal Proceedings -v- M Lucien Gleyzes (Sale of unapproved Telecommunications equipment - Directive 88/301) Removed from the Register 6.12.94).

4.	C-323/91: Ministere Public -v- Alain Marchandeau (Sale of unapproved cordless telephones - Directive 88/301. Removed from the Register 6.12.94).

5.	C-46/93: Firma Brasserie du Pêcheur SA -v- Germany represented by the Minister of Health (Concerning Article 5 and Article 30 of the EEC Treaty. (Joined with C-48/93)).

6.	C-70/93: Bayerische Motorenwerke AG -v- Ald Autoleasing D GMBH (Article 85 EEC Treaty: motor vehicle manufacturer: distribution system).

7.	C-266/93: Bundeskartellamt -v- 1. Volkswagen AG. 2. V.A.G.Leasing GMBH Intervener: V.A.G. - Handlerbeirat E.V. (Article 85(1) EEC Treaty: restrictions on leasing arrangements imposed by Volkswagen on authorised dealers).

8.	C-279/93: Finanzamt Koln-Altstadt -v- Roland Schumaker (German income tax - Belgian national - Article 48 EEC Treaty. Judgment 14.2.95. See Part 2 of this appendix).

9.	C-317/93: Inge Nolte -v- Landesversicherungsanstalt Hannover (Directive 79/7: exclusion of employment involving less than 15 hours per week from the statutory insurance scheme whether sex discrimination if more women than men are affected).

10.	C-340/93: Klaus Thierschmidt GmbH -v- Hauptzollamt Essen (Regulation 4134/86 on the arrangements for imports of certain textile products originating in Taiwan).

11.	C-358/93: Criminal Proceedings -v- Aldo Bordessa (Whether the requirement to make a declaration or receive authorization to remove a specified amount of money from a member state is incompatible with Articles 30,59 or 67 EEC Treaty or Directive 88/ 361/ EEC. Judgment 23.2.95. See Part 2 of this appendix).

12.	C-384/93: Alpine Investments BV -v- Minister Van Financien) (Article 59 EEC Treaty: Provision of financial services. Judgment 10.5.95. See Part 2 of this appendix).

13.	C-397/93: Voltri Terminal Europa SpA -v- Giorgio Donati and Others Interveners: CAP - Consorzio Autonomo Porto Di Genova, CULMV - Compagnia Unica Fra I Lavoratori Delle Mercie Varie. (Dock labour scheme: Articles 90 (1), 30 and 85 EEC Treaty).

14.	C-400/93: Specialarbejderforbundet i Danmark -v- Industriens Arbejdsgivere, Acting On Behalf Of Royal Copenhagen A/S (Article 119 EEC Treaty and Directive 75/117: piece-work systems).(Judgment 31.5.95. See Part 2 of this appendix).

15.	C-416/93: Ministerio Fiscal -v- Vicente Mari Mellado and Concepcion Barbero Maestre (Whether the requirement to make a declaration or receive authorization to remove a specified amount of money from a member state is incompatible with articles 30,59,67 EEC Treaty or Directive 88/361/EEC. Judgment 23.2.95. See Part 2 of this appendix).

16.	C-425/93: Firma Calle Grenzshop Andresen GMBH & Co. KG -v- Allgemeine Ortskrandendasse für de Kreis Schleswig-Flensburg (Regulation 1408/71: Status of Form E101 which certifies the applicable Social Security Scheme for migrant workers. Judgment 16.2.95).

17.	C-427/93, 429/93, 436/93: Bristol Myers Squibb & Others -v- Paranova A/S ET AL (The interpretation of the first Council Directive 89/104/EEC of 21 December 1988 to approximate the laws of the member states relating to trade marks).

18.	C-430/93 and 431/93: 1) J.Van Schijndel 2) J.N.C. Van Veen -v- Stichting

Pensioenfonds Voor Fysiotherapeuten ((i) National measures providing for compulsory membership of an occupational pension scheme and whether Articles 85,86 and 90 EC Treaty apply to such an arrangement. (ii) Whether a national court is obliged to take a point of community law in the absence of such a plea by an interested party and the role of a national court of cassation).

19.   C-434/93: A. Bozkurt -v- Staassecretaris Van Justitie (A Turkish worker; legal employment; work permit, residence permit. Judgment 6.6.95. See Part 2 of this appendix).

20.   C-435/93: Francina Johanna Dietz -v- Stichting Thuiszorg Rotterdam (Article 119 EC and occupational pensions).

21.   C-444/93: Ursula Megner & H Scheffel -v- Innungskrankenkasse Vorderpfalz (Directive 79/7: exclusion of certain workers from compulsory insurance).

22.   C-449/93: Rockfon A/S -v- Specialarbejderforbundet I Danmark Action On Behalf Of Soren Nielsen & Others (Directive 75/129 - collective redundancies.

23.   C-450/93: DIPL.-ING. Eckhard Kalanke -v- Freie Hansestadt Bremen) (Council Directive 76/207: positive discrimination in favour of women).

24.   C-458/93: Mostafa Saddik (Frontier duties on importation of cigarettes - Italian tobacco monopoly- Articles 30,85, 86,and 90 EC Treaty. Order of 23.3.95 declaring reference inadmissible).

25.   C-465/93 & C-466/93: Atlanta Fruchthandelsgesellschaft mbh and 17 Others -v- Federal Republic Of Germany (Allocation of provisional quotas for the import of bananas, interim relief).

26.   C-475/93: Jean-Louis Thevenon and Stadt Speyer-Sozialmat -v- Landesversicherungsanstalt Rheinland-Pfalz (Regulation 1408/71 - Franco-German bilateral social security convention).

27.   C-2/94: Denkavit International BV and Others -v- Kamer Van Koophaandel En Fabrielen Voor Miden Gelderland and others (Directive 69/335 concerning indirect taxes on the raising of capital).

28.   C-55/94: Reinhard Gebhard -v- Consiglio Dell'ordine Degli Avvocati e Procuratori Di Milanom (Directive 77/249 to facilitate the effective exercise by lawyers of freedom to provide services).

29.   C-70/94: Firma Fritz Werner Industrie -v- Germany (German Control of Goods: Article 11 of Regulation 2603/69 establishing Common Rules for Exports).

30.   C-71/94, C-72/94 and C-73/94: Eurim-Pharm Arzneinmittel GmbH -v- Beiersdorf AG and Others (Directive 89/104/EEC: Trademarks and repackaging of pharmaceutical products).

31.   C-83/94: Criminal Proceedings -v- Peter Leifer and others (German Control of Goods: Regulation 2603/69 establishing Common Rules for Exports).

32.   *C-85/94: PIAGEME and Others -v- BVBA Peters (Council Directive 79/112 - labelling of foodstuffs).

33.   C-90/94: Haar Petroleum Ltd -v- Aabenbdraa Havn and others (Articles 9-13,84(2) and 95 of the EEC Treaty: Import surcharge on goods from another member state-limitation period - Emmott).

34. C-96/94: Centro Servizi Spediporto Srl -v- Spedizioni Maritima Del Golfo Srl (Articles 3(f), 5, 30, 85, 86 & 90 of the Treaty: fixing tariffs for carriage of goods by road).

35. C-103/94: Zoulika Krid -v- Caisse Nationale D'Assurance Vieillesse Des Travaillesurs Sslaries (EC/Algeria Co-operation Agreements: entitlement to 'FNS' allowances. Judgment of 5.4.95).

36. C-128/94: Hans Hönig -v- Stadt Stockach (Directive 88/166: Minimum cage area).

37. C-129/94: Ministerio Fiscal -v- Rafael Ruiz (Council directives relating to motor insurance; validity of contractual clauses or Statutory provisions removing insurance cover where the driver was intoxicated).

38. C-134/94: Esso Española -v- Administracion De La Comunidad Autonoma de Canarias (Requirements for the supply of petroleum products in the Canary Islands: Articles 3(c), 52, 7, 53, 85 & 30 EC).

39. C-144/94: Ufficio Iva Di Trapani -v- Soc. Italittica Spa (Article 10(2) of the Sixth Vat Directive).

40. C-152/94: Openbaarr Ministerie -v- Geert R.J.S. Van Buynder (Right of establishment: veterinary operations).

41. C-171/94 and C-172/94: Albert Merckx and Patrick Neuhuys -v- SA Ford Motors Company Belgium (Transfer of undertakings: Directive 77/187).

42. C-178/94, 179/94, 188/94, 189/93 and 190/94: Eric Dillenkofer and Others -v- Bundesrepublic Deutschland (Directive 90/314 on package travel, package holidays and package tours (references to Francovich)).

43. C-193/94: Criminal Proceedings -v- 1) Sofia Skanavi 2) Konstantin Chryssanthakopoulos (Requirement for EC drivers to obtain German driving licence within one year of taking up residence in Germany and the proportionality of the penalties imposed for failure to do so).

44. C-194/94: SA C.I.A. Security International -v- SA Signalson and SPRL Securitel (National provision for approving alarm systems & networks: Article 30 EC: and Directive 83/189 technical standards-effect of failure to notify).

45. C-230/94: Renate Enkler -v-Finanzamt Homburg (Sixth VAT Directive).

46. *C-287/94: Frederiksen -v- Skattemsteriet (Directive 69/335 concerning indirect taxes on the raising of capital).

47. *C-293/94: Openbaar Ministerie -v- Brandsma (Importation of fungicides and national authorisation systems).

48. *C-299/94: Anglo-Irish Beef Processors International -v- Minister for Agriculture (Commission Regulation 3665/87/EEC on export refunds - force majeure - inter-relationship with sanctions against Iraq - Council Regulation 2340/90).

49. *C-313/94: Ayse Suzen -v- Firma Zehmcker Gebandereiniging (Directive 77/187: safeguarding of employee's rights with respect of a transfer of a business).

50. *C-316/94: Etat Belge -v- Turner (Directive 89/552 - pursuit of television broadcasting activities).

51.   *C-355/94: Criminal Proceedings -v- Mrozek & Jager (Regulation 3820/95 - Drivers' Hours. Scope of exception in favour of vehicle used for refuse collection).

52.   *C-1/95: Hellen Gerster -v- Freostaat Bayern (Article 119 and Equal Pay and Equal Treatment Directives : indirect discrimination : rules for calculating seniority of part-time workers).

53.   *C-2/95: Sparerassernes Datacenter -v- Ministry for Fiscal Affairs (Sixth VAT Directive: scope of exclusion of banking services: anciliary activities such as data processing).

54.   *C-39/95: Ministere Public -v- Goupil (Regulation 3820/95: Drivers' Hours : scope of exception in favour of vehicles used for refuse collection).

55.   *C-313/95: Graffione -v- Ditta Fransa (Directive 89/104 - Trade Marks).

(v) Actions in which the United Kingdom intervened in The Court of Justice under Article 37 of the Protocol on the Statute of the Court of Justice.

1.   C-431/92: Commission -v- Germany (Directive 85/337 on the assessment of the effects of certain public & private projects on the environment: construction of a new power station block).

2.   C-65/93: Parliament -v- Council (Application to annul Regulation 3917/92 relating to generalised tariff preferences for 1991 in respect of certain products originating in developing country: consultation procedures. Judgment 30.3.95. See Part 2 of this appendix).

3.   C-74/93 and C-75/93: Commission -v- Council (Application to annul Council decision 92/609 concerning the conclusion of agreements between the EEC and Hungary whether correct legal basis used).

4.   C-296/93: French Republic -v- Commission (An application by France to declare void Regulation 685/93 amending 859/89 laying down maximum carcase weight for eligibility for beef intervention).

5.   C-307/93: Republic of Ireland -v- Commission (An application by the Republic of Ireland to declare void Regulation (EEC) No 685/93 amending 859/89 laying down maximum carcase weight for eligibility for beef intervention).

6.   C-360/93: European Parliament -v- Council (An application to annul Council Decision 93/323/EEC on the conclusion of an Agreement in the form of a memorandum of understading between the EEC and USA on public procurment; whether Article 113 of the EEC treaty as the sole legal basis is correct).

7.   C-445/93: European Parliament -v- Commission (Free movement of persons: Article 7A EC Treaty).

8.   C-21/94: European Parliament -v- Council (An application to declare void Council Directive 93/89 EEC on the basis that the Parliament should have been reconsulted).

9.   C-25/94: Commission -v- Council (Fisheries Council Decision of 22 November 1993 on voting within the U.N. Food and Agriculture Organisation. (FAO))

10.   C-74/94: France -v- Commission (Regulation 2408/92: - application to annul Commission Decision 94/290 EEC that the French policy on the distribution of traffic between airports result in discrimination based on the nationaliy of air carriers).

11.   C-156/94: Commission -v- Ireland (Articles 30, 34 & 37: State monopoly in respect of the import and export of electricity).

12.   C-157/94: Commission -v- Netherlands (Articles 30, 34 & 37: State monopoly in respect of the import electricity).

13.   *C-158/94: Commission -v- Italy (Articles 30, 34 & 37: State monopoly in respect of the import and export of electricity).

14.   C-159/94: Commission -v- France (Articles 30, 34 & 37: State monopolies in respect of the import and export of gas and electricity).

15.   C-160/94: Commission -v- Spain (Articles 30, 34 & 37: State monopoly in respect of the import and export of electricity).

16.   C-174/94: France -v- Commission (An application by France to annul Commission Decision 93/291/EEC that France should not continue to refuse Community air carriers traffic rights on the Paris-Marseille/Toulouse routes on the ground that France was applying Article 5 of Regulation 2408/92 to these routes).

(17.   C-203/94: France -v- Commission (Regulation 2408/92: application to annul commission Decision 94/290/EEC that the French policy on the distribution of traffic between airports results in discrimination based on the nationality of air carriers).

18.   *C-268/94: Portugal -v- Council (Co-operation Agreement between the EC and India on Partnership and Development).

19.   C-301/94: Air Inter -v- Commission (Regulation 2408/92: application to annul commission Decision 94/290/EEC that the French policy on the distribution of traffic between airports results in discrimination based on the nationality of air carriers).

(vi) Actions in which the United Kingdom intervened in the Court of First Instance under Article 37 of the Protocol on the Statute of the Court of Justice).

1.   T-247/93: Stenhouse -v- Council and Commission (Milk Producer claiming damages due to refusal of milk quota. Transferred from ECJ: C-122/92).

2.   T-357/93: W.J. WYNESSS -v- Council & Commission (Milk producer claiming damages).

3.   T-517/93: N.V.Leon Van Parijs and Others -v- Council (Action for damages/annulment of Regulation 404/93 (the common organisation of the market in bananas). Partially removed from Register 6.3.95).

4.   T-518/93: Anton Durbeck -v- Council (Action for damages/annulment of Regulation 404/93 (the common organisation of the market in bananas). Removed from Register 28.3.95).

5.   T-519/93: Comafrica and Others -v- Council (Action for damages/annulment of Regulation 404/93 (the common organisation of the market in bananas). Removed from Register 20.3.95).

6.   T-520/93: Pacific Fruit -v- Council (Action for damages/annulment of Regulation 404/93 (the common organisation of the market in bananas). Removed from Register 14.2.95).

7.   T-521/93: Atlanta Aktiengesellschaft & Others -v- Council (Action for damages/annulment of Regulation 404/93 (the common organisation of the market in bananas)).

8.   T-529/93: Rodgers & Other 3 -v- Council & Commission (Milk Producers).

9.   *T-541/93: Coughlin & 2 Others -v- Council & Commission (Milk producers).

10.   T-454/93, T-455/93, T-456/93, T-457/93 : Elders & others -v- Commission. (Formerly C-355/92, C-356/92, C-347/92 & C-370/92) - An application to declare void Regulation 1922/92, relating to variable slaughter premium for sheep and amend the amount of clawback).

11.   *T-555/93: Jones & Jones & Others -v- Council & Commission

12.   T-70/94: Comafrica Spa & Dole Fresh Fruit -v- Commission (Regulation 3190/93 concerning import of bananas).

13.   T-371/94: B A -v- Commission (State Aids : Air France).

14.   *T-394/94: British Middlands Air Ways Ltd -v- Commission (State Aids : Air France).

(vii) Cases referred to the European Court under the Judgments Convention.

1.   C-68/93: Shevill and Others -v- Presse Alliance S. A. (Brussels Convention : Libel by a newspaper article. Judgment 7.3.95).
2.   C-341/93: Danvaern Production A/S -v- Schuhfabriken Otterbeck GmbH & Co (Brussels Convention: Article 6 (3): Counterclaims).

3.   C-346/93: Kleinwort Benson Limited -v- City of Glasgow District Council (Brussels Convention: local authority "SWAPS" agreements. Judgment 28.3.95).

4.   C-364/93: Antonio Marinari -v- Lloyds Bank plc and Zubaidi Trading Company. (Article 5 (3) of the Brussels Convention and the meaning of ("place where the harmful event occurred").

5.   C-432/93: Societe D' Informatique Service Realisation Organisation-SISRO -v- Ampersand Software BV and Others (Articles 36-38 of the Brussels Convention-recognition of judgment).

6.   C-439/93: The Lloyd's Register of Shipping -v- Societe Campenon Bernard (Article 5 of the Brussels Convention. Judgment 6.4.95).

(viii) Requests for an Opinion of the European Court of Justice under Article 228(1) of the EEC Treaty

1.   Opinion 2/92 (Request by Belgium for an Opinion. Third Revised Decision of the OECD on National Treatment: correct legal basis. Opinion delivered on 24.3.95. See Part 2 of this appendix).

2.   Opinion 2/94 (Request for an opinion Submitted by the Council on accession by the Community to the European Convention on Human Rights).

3.   Opinion 3/94 (Request for an Opinion submitted by Germany. Compatibility of the provisions of the Framework Agreement on Bananas of 28/29 March 1994 with the Treaty establishing the European Community (Article 228(6) of the EC Treaty and Article 107 the Rules of Procedure of the Court of Justice).

(ix) Actions against United Kingdom under Article 170.

None.

Appendix D, Part 2: Summary of important Judgments

ECJ Opinion 2/92: OECD Third Decision on National Treatment (Opinion 24 March)

1.   In this case (following a request by Belgium) the ECJ was asked to give its opinion on whether the Community had exclusive competence to participate in the OECD's Third Decision on National Treatment.

2.   The Third Decision forms part of the Strengthened National Treatment Instrument under which undertakings owned or controlled by nationals of one OECD member country are to be accorded, when operating in the territory of another member country, treatment which is no less favourable than that which is accorded in like situations to domestic undertakings. It was argued that this was an area covered by the common commercial policy for which the Community had exclusive competence under Article 113.

3.   The Court concluded that Article 113 did not confer exclusive competence here given that the national treatment rule affected intra-Community trade to the same extent as international trade, if not more so: intra-Community trade is governed by the Community's internal market rules and not those of its common commercial policy. Nor did the Community have exclusive competence by virtue of the internal Community rules that would be affected. It was undisputed that such measures did not cover all the fields of activity to which the Third Decision relates.

4.   The importance of this decision lies in its description of the circumstances in which the Community has exclusive competence to undertake obligations to third countries.

ECJ Case 65/93: Parliament v Council (Judgment 30 March)

1.   This case concerns the Parliament's application for annulment of Regulation 3917/92 on generalised tariff preferences. The Council referred the proposal to the Parliament for its opinion in accordance with the consultation procedure. It asked the Parliament to apply the urgency procedure under its Rules of Procedure. When the Parliament adjourned debate on the proposal for a month, without holding an extraordinary session, the Council adopted the regulation without waiting for the Parliament's opinion. The Parliament argued that this was a breach of an essential procedural requirement.

2.   The Court dismissed the application, although it held that consultation was an essential procedural requirement. In an emergency, it is for the Council to use all possibilities available under the Treaty and Rules of Procedure to obtain the Parliament's opinion. The Parliament, however, had failed in its duty of sincere co-operation to the other institutions in adjourning the debate for reasons unconnected with the regulation and in failing to take account of the urgency and accordingly could not complain that it had been adopted without consultation.

3.   The case is important because it makes clear that there are circumstances in the consultation procedure in which the Council need not await the Parliament's opinion.

ECJ Case C279/93: Roland Schumacker v Finanzamt Köln-Altstadt (Judgment 14 February)

1.   In this case the ECJ was asked to consider whether certain national tax rules treating resident and non-resident workers differently were incompatible with the right of free movement under EC law.

2.   The case concerned a Belgian national resident in Belgium. He worked in Germany as an employee and was treated as a non-resident taxpayer. This meant that he was not entitled to allowances and reliefs available under German income tax rules to take into account personal and family circumstances, including the privilege of the spousal splitting income tax rate. Because his salary was taxable only in Germany and because he had no other taxable income his personal and family circumstances were not able to be taken into account for tax purposes in Belgium either. He complained that the German tax rules treating non-residents less favourably than residents amounted to disguised discrimination on the grounds of nationality, because non-residents are normally foreign nationals, and that this adversely affected his freedom of movement under Article 48 of the Treaty.

3.   The Court noted that national tax rules distinguishing between residents and non-residents were not, in general, incompatible with EC law. It ruled however that where non-resident workers exercise rights of free movement under the Treaty, the state where they work is required to tax them in the same way as residents if the non-resident worker receives all or almost all his income from working in that state and receives insufficient income from his state of residence to be taxed there in a way which allows his personal and family circumstances to be taken into account.

4.   The importance of the case is that it has resolved the issue of the tax treatment of individuals who live in one member state and work in another. This is of particular significance for those member states in which cross-border commuting is commonplace.

ECJ Case C-324/93: R v Secretary of State for the Home Department ex parte Evans Medical Ltd and Macfarlan Smith Ltd, intervener: Generics (UK) Ltd. (Judgment 28 March)

1.   In this case the ECJ was asked to clarify the interaction of controls on the licit trade in narcotic drugs as found in domestic and international law with the trade provisions of the Treaty of Rome.

2.   In 1992 following a legal challenge by Generics (UK) Ltd, the Home Department amended the longstanding ban on the importation of narcotic drugs by allowing the company to import a quantity of diamorphine (medical heroin) from the Netherlands. This decision was in turn challenged by Macfarlan Smith Ltd (MSL), the sole UK manufacturer of narcotic drugs, and by Evans Medical Ltd (Evans), the then sole processor of diamorphine. They contended that compliance with the United Nations Single Convention on Narcotic Drugs 1961 was incompatible with Articles 30 and 36 of the Treaty of Rome.

3.   In its judgment the ECJ confirmed that Article 30 was applicable to a policy prohibiting imports from other member states and that the derogation provided in Article 36 for the protection, health and life of humans was available provided it was based on protecting a reliable supply of essential drugs; it was not available for safeguarding an

undertaking's survival. As a pre-existing commitment to non member states, the Convention could potentially justify a control which would otherwise fall foul of Article 30, but only if the control was necessary to ensure compliance with the Convention.

4.   The case is significant in confirming the applicability of the provisions of European Union law against restrictive practices in the intra-Community trade in narcotic drugs. It also points up the possibly anomalous position of other member states who produce narcotics.

ECJ Joined Cases C358/93 and C416/93, Ministerio Fiscal v Aldo Bordessa and others (Judgment 23 February)

1.   In this case the ECJ was asked to consider the compatibility with EC law of rules of Spanish law requiring that the export of coins, banknotes or bearer cheques be conditional upon prior declaration or administrative authorisation.

2.   Mr Bordessa was caught by French police with 50 million Spanish pesetas concealed in special compartments of a Mercedes Benz 300D car. He was returned to the Spanish authorities who prosecuted him. It is an offence under Spanish law to export more than 1 million pesetas in cash without making an official declaration. If one wants to export more than 5 million pesetas in cash one must receive official authorisation.

3.   The UK's concern was to ensure that any judgment from the ECJ did not cast doubt on the national regime put in place by the Criminal Justice (International Co-operation) Act 1990 whereby cash over £10,000 being exported from or imported into the UK could be detailed pending inquiry and forfeited upon proof that it represented the proceeds of drug trafficking.

4.   The Court ruled that EC law precludes member states from requiring a prior administrative authorisation as a condition of exporting coins, banknotes or bearer cheques.

5.   However, the importance of the case stems from the remarks in the Court's judgment that member states may nevertheless take measures to prevent illegality in the tax system, to supervise financial institutions and to prevent money laundering, drug trafficking, terrorism and other serious illegal activities.

ECJ Case C384/93: Alpine Investments BV v Minister Van Financien (Judgment 10 May)

1.   In this case the ECJ was asked to consider the extent to which a member state is entitled to regulate the offer of services from its territory to a potential recipient established in another member state.

2.   The case concerned a financial intermediary established in the Netherlands, who was prevented by a Dutch ban on cold-calling from telephoning potential clients in other member states. The intermediary complained that the ban was incompatible with the freedom to provide services under Article 59.

3.   The ECJ held that such a problem on cold-calling deprived the operators concerned of a rapid and direct technique for marketing and contracting potential clients in other member states and could therefore fall foul of Article 59. However, the Court held that the nature and extent of the protection of consumers in other member states had a direct effect on the good reputation of Dutch financial services. Given that the cold-calling concerned services linked to investment in commodities futures, such a ban might be justified in order to protect investor confidence in the national financial market.

4.   The case illustrates that the freedom to provide such services may be restricted as much by barriers imposed by the State of origin as those imposed by the State of destination. Its importance also lies in the recognition that maintaining the good reputation of the national financial sector may justify such restrictions provided they are no more restrictive of cross-border services than necessary.

ECJ Case C400/93: Special Arbejderforbundet i Danmark (Union of Semi-Skilled Workers in Denmark) v Dansk Industri (Confederation of Danish Industry) acting for Royal Copenhagen A/S (Judgment 31 May)

1.   In this case the ECJ was asked whether the principle of equal pay applies to piece work schemes; if so, whether the comparison should be between the average hourly pay of two groups, one consisting mainly of men, the other mainly of women, assumed to be performing work of equal value. The Court was also asked by what criteria the composition of the groups must be determined.

2.   The Court held that pieceworkers could bring equal pay claims but, since the rationale behind piecework was to pay more to more productive workers, the mere fact that there were differences in average pay did not demonstrate discrimination. The "unit of measurement" for the work of the two groups must either be the same or, where the work of the two groups was different but of equal value, be objectively capable of ensuring that total pay was the same. It was for the national court to decide whether this was so and to ascertain whether any differences were objectively justified. The employer may have to show that differences were not due to sex discrimination.

3.   The groups must encompass all the workers in a comparable situation to ensure that mere fortuitous or short-term factors or differences of individual output were not distorting pay levels.

ECJ Case 417/93: Parliament v Council (Judgment 10 May)

1.   In this case the Parliament applied for annulment of Regulation 2053/93 concerning the TACIS programme. The Parliament complained that by the time the proposal, which was subject to the consultation procedure, was officially referred to it, the Council had already discussed and in effect decided on the substance of the regulation, so that consultation was a sham. It also complained that the proposal was amended after the Parliament had given its opinion, but that the Council had not re-consulted the Parliament.

2.   The Court dismissed the application. It held that nothing in Community law requires the Council to abstain from considering a proposal before the Parliament delivers its opinion so long as it does not adopt a final position before receiving an opinion. In this case none of the amendments to the text (including a change of the type of committee to be used) constituted a substantial amendment requiring re-consultation of the Parliament. Finally, it was lawful for the regulation to include provision for its amendment by the Council without consulting the Parliament: the consultation procedure applied only to the adoption of the basic regulation.

3.   This case builds on Case 65/93 (see above), clarifying the extent of the obligation to consult the Parliament and resisting attempts by the Parliament to extend its role in the consultation procedure.

ECJ Case C4/94: BLP plc v The Commissioners of Customs and Excise (Judgment 6 April)

1.   In this case the ECJ was asked to consider a rule relating to permissible deductions for the purposes of Value Added Tax (VAT).

2.   A trader received professional services and used them in connection with its sale of shares in a subsidiary company. The fees for those services included VAT. It sought to deduct that VAT. If the services were used solely for the sale of shares then no such deduction would have been allowed (since the supply of shares is exempt for the purposes of VAT and input tax attributable to exempt supplies is not generally deductible).

3.   However, the cash raised by the sale of shares assisted the trader in its core business of making taxable supplies of goods (ie supplies subject to VAT). If, therefore, the services were also used for those supplies of goods rather than used solely for the sale of shares a deduction would have been allowable.

4.   The Court held that services purchased and used in making an exempt supply leading to the making of a taxable supply are nevertheless only used for that exempt supply and not for the taxable supply. Accordingly there is no entitlement to a deduction of the VAT charged on the fees for those services.

5.   The importance of the case lies in its clarification of the extent to which traders may be entitled to a deduction of VAT in circumstances such as these.

ECJ Case C434/93: Bozkurt v Staatssecretaris Von Justitie (Judgment 6 June)

1.   This case concerned a request by a Turkish national for an unlimited residence permit in the Netherlands under provisions relating to the Association Agreement between the European Economic Community and Turkey. The provisions entitle, inter alia, a Turkish national who is duly registered as belonging to the labour force of a member state to any paid employment of his choice, after four years of paid employment.

2.   The applicant had been employed as an international lorry driver since 1979 by a company based in the Netherlands. Between journeys and while on leave he lived in the Netherlands. In 1988 the applicant suffered an accident at work and was permanently incapacitated for work. He received benefits under Netherlands law. He applied for an unrestricted residence permit in 1991 but this was refused.

3.   The Court was concerned with three main questions: whether the applicant's employment as an international lorry driver in the service of a Netherlands company resulted in him being a member of the labour force in the Netherlands; if he did not need a work permit or a residence permit, and could not acquire a long-term residence permit under Netherlands law because of the usually short periods he remained in the Netherlands, did the applicant have a right of residence under the provisions relating to the Association Agreement; and, if so, did he retain that right if he became permanently and completely incapable of work?

4.   The Court held that it was for the national court to decide whether the applicant maintained a sufficiently close link in the Netherlands to be a legitimate member of the labour force. The fact that under Netherlands law he did not require a work permit or residence permit did not preclude his being in legal employment and being entitled therefore to reside in the Netherlands. The issue of administrative documents would only be declaratory of his rights and not a condition for their existence.

5.   However, the Court also held that the Association Agreement and related provision do not give a Turkish national a right to reside in a member state when his incapacity means that he is no longer available as a member of the labour force. The rights of those who are temporarily absent from work are preserved by specific provisions which do not extend to those permanently incapacitated for work.

Appendix E: House of Commons Debates on European Community Documents

a. Floor of the House

Date		Subject and Document References
1.	21 March	Prices for Agricultural Products and on related measures (1995-1996) (1). (5097/93, Vol I-III)

b. European Standing Committee A

1.	25 January	Production Refund on certain Sugar Products used in the Chemical Industry (11141/94)
2.	1 February	Recording Equipment in Road Transport (8958/94)
3.	29 March	Inter-operability of the European high speed train network (6495/94 & Supp. EM of 24/2/95)
4.	23 May	Aid for Cotton (5489/95 (covered by Ministerial letter dated 4/5/95))
5.	13 June	Management of Fishing Effort (U/N EM of 6/6/95)

c. European Standing Committee B

1.	1 February	(Protocol on Social Policy (4075/94) ((Informing and Consulting Employees ((6230/94) ((European Social Policy - A way forward (for the Union - A White Paper (9069/94)
2.	15 February	Euro-Mediterranean Association Agreement with Israel (U/N EM of 9/12/94)
3.	22 February	Budgetizing the European Development Fund (7854/94)
4.	28 February	Co-operation Agreement with Russia (7988/94, U/N EM of 27/1/95)
5.	1 March	Temporary Postings of Workers (7484/93)
6.	8 March	Court of Auditors Report (U/N EM 23/11/94)

7.	15 March	Hallmarking (9508/93 & Supp EM of 9/6/95, 8251/94)
8.	22 March	External Frontiers (11287/93)
9.	29 March	Protection of Community Financial Interests (8076/94 Pts 1 & 2)
10.	26 April	Adjusting Accession Instrument (U/N EM of 13/12/94)
11.	10 May	(Green paper on telecommunications ((10589/94) ((Telecommunications Infrastructure ((4674/94) ((Telecommunications (U/N EM if 28/4/95)
12.	17 May	Green paper: energy policy (4523/95 + Supp. EM of 28/2/95)
13.	24 May	(Relations with Central and Eastern (Europe (8693/94 & Supp EM of 12/12/94, (8943/94) ((Industrial Co-operation with Central (and Eastern Europe (5928/95)
14.	7 June	Consumer Protection (4069/95 & Supp EM of 10/3/95)
15.	14 June	Broad Economic Guidelines (U/N EM of 6/6/95)
16.	21 June	Economic Growth and the Environment (10911/94)

Appendix F: Reports from the House of Lords Select Committee on the European Communities

a. Reports Presented for Debate

Subject and Document References	Report No. and date
1. Reform of the EC Sugar Regime (11141/94 + Supp. EM)	4th Report 1994-95 14 February
2. Bathing Water Revisited, (6177/94)	7th Report 1994-95 21 March
3. European Film and Television Industry (6398/94, 10585/94)	8th Report 1994-95 4 April
4. Europol (9757/93, 12321/1/94 REV 1)	10th Report 1994-95, 25 April
5. Relations between the EU and Maghreb countries (8521/94, 10428/94, 11221/94, 5766/95)	11th Report 1994-95 9 May

b. Reports Presented for Information

1. Essen European Council and Related Matters	3rd Report 1994-95 24 January
2. European Environment Agency	5th Report 1994-95 14 February
3. Correspondence with Ministers	6th Report 1994-95 7 March
4. Veterinary Certification of Animals and Animal products, (12048/94)	9th Report 1994-95 4 April
5. Cross-Border Credit Transfers (11389/94)	12th Report 1994/95 13 June

c. Debates Held

1. Sugar Regime - Referendum of EC (11141/94 + Supp EM)	4th Report 1994/95 the 23 March
2. Bathing Water and Bathing Water Revisited (6177/94)	1st Report 1994/95 7th Report 1994/95 18 May
3. EUROPOL (9757/93, 12321/1/94 REV 1)	10th Report 1994/95 6 June

Appendix G: United Kingdom Trade with the European Community

Note: All the figures in the Following text and the accompanying table incorporate statistics of trade with Austria, Finland and Sweden. All figures are on a balance of payments basis.

Importance of Trade with the Community

Nearly 60 per cent of the United Kingdom's trade (exports plus imports) is now with other member states, compared with about 40 per cent prior to United Kingdom membership. In recent years Germany has become our most important trading partner and eight of our top ten markets are members of the Community.

Trade Performance in the Community

In the first half of 1995 United Kingdom trade with other member states amounted to £88.5 billion compared with £76.2 billion in the first half of 1994. Exports grew by 17 per cent while imports grew by 15 per cent.

By Commodity

In January to June 1995 exports of fuels (mainly oil) accounted for nearly 8 per cent of our total exports to other member states, little changed from the same period a year earlier but well below the figure of nearly 30 per cent in the mid-1980s. This declining share can be some extent be explained by weaker oil prices in recent years. The surplus on fuels rose by £0.4 billion to £2.5 billion.

The deficit on manufactured goods fell by £0.1 billion to £2.7 billion.

UNITED KINGDOM TRADE WITH THE EUROPEAN COMMUNITY £ billion, Balance of Payments Basis

	Total Trade				Food, Beverages and Tobacco				Basic Materials			
	Exports	Imports	Balance	Export/Import Ratio %	Exports	Imports	Balance	Export/Import Ratio %	Exports	Imports	Balance	Export/Import Ratio%
1970	3.2	3.1	+0.1	104	0.1	0.8	-0.6	19	0.2	0.3	-0.1	63
1971	3.4	3.6	-0.2	94	0.2	0.9	-0.7	18	0.2	0.3	-0.1	66
1972	3.8	4.6	-0.8	83	0.2	1.0	-0.8	21	0.2	0.3	-0.1	68
1973	5.0	6.7	-1.7	74	0.3	1.4	-1.1	22	0.3	0.5	-0.2	59
1974	7.1	9.7	-2.6	73	0.3	2.0	-1.7	14	0.4	0.6	-0.2	61
1975	7.9	10.5	-2.7	75	0.5	2.4	-1.9	21	0.4	0.6	-0.2	67
1976	11.1	13.6	-2.5	81	0.6	2.5	-1.9	25	0.6	0.9	-0.3	68
1977	14.2	16.3	-2.1	87	0.9	2.9	-2.0	31	0.7	1.0	-0.3	69
1978	15.8	18.6	-2.8	85	1.3	3.1	-1.8	41	0.7	0.9	-0.2	76
1979	20.4	23.5	-3.0	87	1.4	3.4	-2.1	40	0.9	1.1	-0.2	82
1980	24.2	23.2	+0.9	104	1.5	3.3	-1.8	45	1.1	1.0	+0.1	106
1981	24.4	24.6	-0.2	99	1.6	3.6	-2.0	44	0.9	1.1	-0.3	78
1982	27.1	28.6	-1.5	95	1.7	4.0	-2.3	43	1.0	1.3	-0.3	76
1983	31.2	34.3	-3.0	91	1.8	4.6	-2.7	40	1.1	1.5	-0.4	76
1984	36.9	40.7	-3.7	91	1.9	5.1	-3.1	38	1.5	1.9	-0.4	77
1985	42.1	44.9	-2.8	94	2.1	5.5	-3.4	38	1.6	1.9	-0.3	83
1986	38.3	48.4	-10.1	79	2.7	6.3	-3.6	43	1.5	1.9	-0.4	79
1987	42.6	53.8	-11.2	79	2.7	6.6	-3.8	41	1.6	2.2	-0.7	71
1988	44.3	60.5	-16.2	73	3.4	7.0	-3.6	48	1.4	2.1	-0.7	66
1989	51.0	68.7	-17.7	74	3.9	7.6	-3.7	51	1.6	2.3	-0.7	68
1990	58.6	70.3	-11.7	83	4.0	7.8	-3.8	51	1.6	2.5	-0.9	65
1991	62.9	65.3	-2.4	96	4.8	7.8	-3.0	62	1.3	2.2	-0.8	62
1992	64.7	69.7	-4.9	93	5.5	8.5	-3.1	64	1.2	2.3	-1.0	55
1993	68.9	74.3	-5.4	93	5.5	8.7	-3.2	63	1.4	2.4	-1.0	58
1994	76.5	82.1	-5.6	93	6.2	9.1	-2.9	68	1.7	2.8	-1.1	60
Jan -Jun 94	36.7	39.5	-2.7	93	3.0	4.5	-1.5	67	0.8	1.3	-0.5	60
Jan -Jun 95	43.1	45.4	-2.3	95	3.4	4.9	-1.5	69	1.0	1.4	-0.5	66

	Fuels				Manufactures			
	Exports	Imports	Balance	Export/Import Ratio %	Exports	Imports	Balance	Export/Import Ratio %
1970	0.1	0.2	-0.1	53	2.7	1.8	+0.9	148
1971	0.1	0.3	-0.1	49	2.9	2.2	+0.7	131
1972	0.1	0.3	-0.2	45	3.1	2.9	+0.2	107
1973	0.2	0.4	-0.2	50	4.1	4.3	-0.2	95
1974	0.5	1.1	-0.6	45	5.8	5.9	-0.2	97
1975	0.5	1.1	-0.6	48	6.3	6.4	-0.1	98
1976	0.8	1.4	-0.6	60	8.8	8.6	+0.1	102
1977	1.3	1.4	-0.1	94	11.0	10.8	+0.1	101
1978	1.5	1.3	+0.2	115	12.0	13.1	-1.1	91
1979	3.0	2.0	+1.0	148	14.8	16.8	-1.9	88
1980	4.6	2.0	+2.7	235	16.5	16.7	-0.1	99
1981	6.1	2.1	+4.0	285	15.4	17.4	-2.0	88
1982	7.0	2.2	+4.8	323	17.0	20.8	-3.8	82
1983	9.0	2.2	+6.8	408	18.7	25.6	-6.8	73
1984	10.7	3.4	+7.3	316	22.2	29.8	-7.6	75
1985	12.3	3.3	+9.0	372	25.5	33.6	-8.1	76
1986	6.0	1.9	+4.1	315	27.3	37.7	-10.4	72
1987	6.0	1.9	+4.1	317	31.5	42.5	-11.1	74
1988	4.1	1.7	+2.4	239	34.6	48.7	-14.1	71
1989	4.1	2.0	+2.0	200	40.5	55.7	-15.2	73
1990	5.3	1.9	+3.4	276	46.9	57.4	-10.5	82
1991	5.3	1.9	+3.4	281	50.7	52.7	-2.1	96
1992	4.9	1.7	+3.2	294	52.3	56.4	-4.2	93
1993	5.6	1.6	+4.0	357	56.3	61.4	-5.1	92
1994	5.6	1.4	+4.2	410	63.0	68.7	-5.7	92
Jan-Jun 94	2.7	0.7	+2.1	406	30.1	32.9	-2.8	92
Jan-Jun 95	3.2	0.7	+2.5	467	35.6	38.3	-2.7	93

Printed in the United Kingdom for HMSO
Dd 5067083 11/95 C12 65536 3401/3 45/34002